W9-DIU-878

math
expressions
Common Core

Dr. Karen C. Fuson

 Watch the lemur come alive in its forest as you discover and solve math challenges.

Download the *Math Worlds AR* app available on Android or iOS devices.

Grade 4

Volume 1

This material is based upon work supported by the
National Science Foundation
under Grant Numbers
ESI-9816320, REC-9806020, and RED-935373.

Any opinions, findings, and conclusions, or recommendations expressed in this material
are those of the author and do not necessarily reflect the views of the National Science Foundation.

BIG IDEA 3 - Subtraction with Greater Numbers

Unit 2 | Multiplication with Whole Numbers

BIG IDEA 1 - Multiplication with Tens and Hundreds

BIG IDEA 2 - Multiply by One-Digit Numbers

BIG IDEA 1 - Dividing Whole Numbers

BIG IDEA 2 - Division Issues and Word Problems

Unit 4 | Equations and Word Problems

BIG IDEA 1 - Reasoning and Solving Problems

BIG IDEA 2 - Comparison Word Problems

BIG IDEA 3 - Problems with More Than One Step

BIG IDEA 4 - Analyzing Patterns

Student Resources

addend

greater than
(>)

digit

inverse
operations

expanded
form

less than (<)

A symbol used to compare two numbers.

The greater number is given first below.

Example:
33 > 17
33 is greater than 17.

One of two or more numbers added together to find a sum.

Example:
7 + 8 = 15

addend   addend   sum

Opposite or reverse operations that undo each other. Addition and subtraction are inverse operations. Multiplication and division are inverse operations.

Examples:
4 + 6 = 10 so, 10 − 6 = 4 and
10 − 4 = 6.
3 × 9 = 27 so, 27 ÷ 9 = 3 and 27 ÷ 3 = 9.

Any of the symbols 0, 1, 2, 3, 4, 5, 6, 7, 8, or 9.

A symbol used to compare two numbers.

The smaller number is given first below.

Example:
54 < 78
54 is less than 78.

A way of writing a number that shows the value of each of its digits.

Example:
Expanded form of 835:
800 + 30 + 5
8 hundreds + 3 tens + 5 ones

place value

standard form

word form

The value assigned to the place that a digit occupies in a number.

Example:
235

↑

The 2 is in the hundreds place, so its value is 200.

The form of a number written using digits.

Example:
2,145

The form of a number written using words instead of digits.

Example:
Six hundred thirty-nine

Name Aaron

Model Hundreds

You can represent numbers by making place value drawings on a dot array.

1 What number does this drawing show? 537
   Explain your thinking.

   5 hundreds blocks, 3 tens, 7 cubes!

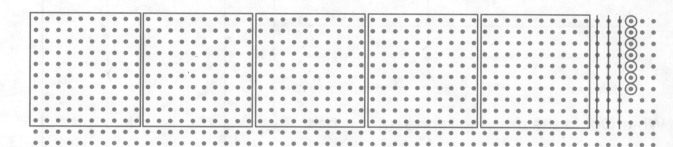

Model Thousands

Discuss this place value drawing. Write the number of each.

2 ones: 8

3 quick tens: 6

4 hundred boxes: 4

5 thousand bars: 3

6 How many hundred boxes could we draw inside each thousand bar? Explain.

7 What number does this drawing show?

   3,463

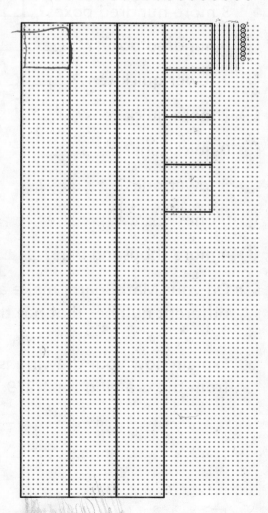

© Houghton Mifflin Harcourt Publishing Company

Model Greater Numbers

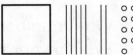

VOCABULARY
place value

Place value can also be shown without using a dot array.

8 What number does this drawing represent? Explain your thinking.

_1,279_

What would the drawing represent if it had:

9 3 more hundred boxes? _1,579_

10 0 hundred boxes? _1,079_

11 2 fewer quick tens? _1,259_

12 2 more quick tens? _1,299_

13 0 quick tens? _1,207_

14 5 fewer ones? _1,274_

15 0 ones? _1,200_

16 4 more thousand bars? _5,279_

17 On your MathBoard, make a place value drawing for a different number that has the digits 1, 2, 7, and 9.

18 Explain how your drawing is similar to and different from the drawing for 1,279.

© Houghton Mifflin Harcourt Publishing Company

Practice with Place Value Drawings

Make a place value drawing for each number, using ones, quick tens, and hundred boxes.

19 6

20 3

21 603

22 300

23 63

24 32

25 325

26 285

27 109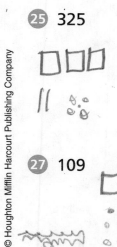

28 573

Practice Modeling Thousands

**Make a place value drawing for each number, using ones,
quick tens, hundred boxes, and thousand bars.**

29 2,596

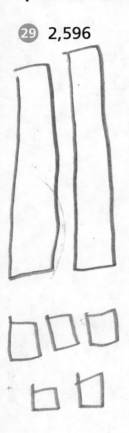

30 3,045

✓ Check Understanding

Make a place value drawing to show 2,361. Then compare
it to the place value drawing for Exercise 29 and explain the
differences between the two drawings.

Place Value to Thousands

1,000 **1,000**	100 **100**
2,000 **2,000**	200 **200**
3,000 **3,000**	300 **300**
4,000 **4,000**	400 **400**
5,000 **5,000**	500 **500**
6,000 **6,000**	600 **600**
7,000 **7,000**	700 **700**
8,000 **8,000**	800 **800**
9,000 **9,000**	900 **900**

Whole Number Secret Code Cards **6A**

one hundred	one thousand
two hundred	two thousand
three hundred	three thousand
four hundred	four thousand
five hundred	five thousand
six hundred	six thousand
seven hundred	seven thousand
eight hundred	eight thousand
nine hundred	nine thousand

Whole Number Secret Code Cards

10	1 0	1	1
20	2 0	2	2
30	3 0	3	3
40	4 0	4	4
50	5 0	5	5
60	6 0	6	6
70	7 0	7	7
80	8 0	8	8
90	9 0	9	9

Whole Number Secret Code Cards **6C**

one	ten (teen) (one ten)
two	twenty (two tens)
three	thirty (three tens)
four	forty (four tens)
five	fifty (five tens)
six	sixty (six tens)
seven	seventy (seven tens)
eight	eighty (eight tens)
nine	ninety (nine tens)

Whole Number Secret Code Cards

The Place Value Chart

Discuss the patterns you see in the Place Value Poster below.

← × 10 (Greater)

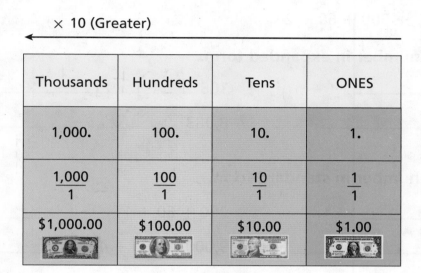

Thousands	Hundreds	Tens	ONES
1,000.	100.	10.	1.
$\frac{1,000}{1}$	$\frac{100}{1}$	$\frac{10}{1}$	$\frac{1}{1}$
$1,000.00	$100.00	$10.00	$1.00

Use your Whole Number Secret Code Cards to make numbers on the frame.

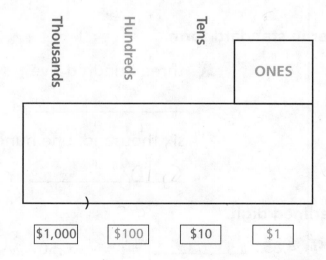

Thousands   Hundreds   Tens   ONES

$1,000 $100 $10 $1

Write Numbers Using Expanded Form

VOCABULARY
standard form
word form
expanded form

Standard form: 8,562

Word form: eight thousand, five hundred sixty-two

Expanded form: 8,000 + 500 + 60 + 2

Read and write each number in expanded form.

1. 73 _70+3_

2. 108 _100+8_

3. 5,621 _5,000 + 600 + 20 + 1_

4. 8,083 _8,000 + 80 + 3_

Read and write each number in standard form.

5. 40 + 3 _43_

6. 200 + 60 + 1 _261_

7. 1,000 + 70 + 9 _1,079_

8. 9,000 + 800 + 4 _9,804_

Read and write each number in word form.

9. 400 + 40 + 1 _four-hundred-fourty-one_

10. 1,000 + 50 _one-thousand-fifty_

Read and write each number in standard form.

11. thirty-five
    _35_

12. three hundred five
    _305_

13. six thousand, eight
    _6,008_

14. six thousand, one hundred eight
    _6,108_

Write the value of the underlined digit.

15. 7<u>5</u>6 _60_

16. <u>4</u>,851 _4,000_

17. 6,<u>5</u>07 _500_

✓ **Check Understanding**

Explain how to use place value to write a number
in standard, word, and expanded forms.

Place Value Patterns

Name _____

Summarize Rounding Rules

Use these rounding frames as a visual aid when rounding to the nearest 1,000; 100; 10.

Nearest 1,000	Nearest 100	Nearest 10
10,000	1,000	100
9,000	900	90
8,000	800	80
7,000	700	70
6,000	600	60
5,000	500	50
4,000	400	40
3,000	300	30
2,000	200	20
1,000	100	10
0	0	0

Round to the nearest thousand.

1 1,275 _5000_   **2** 8,655 _9,000_   **3** 5,482 _5000_

4 3,804 _4000_   **5** 1,501 _200 0_   **6** 9,702 _10,000_

Round to the nearest hundred.

7 734 _____   **8** 363 _____   **9** 178 _____

10 6,249 _6,250_   **11** 8,251 _____   **12** 8,992 _900 0_

Round to the nearest ten.

13 87 _____   **14** 16 _____   **15** 171 _170_

16 2,165 _2,170_   **17** 5,114 _____   **18** 3,098 _____

Compare Numbers

Discuss the problem below.

Jim has 24 trading cards and Hattie has 42 trading cards.
Who has more trading cards? How do you know?

Draw a place value model for each problem.
Write > (greater than), < (less than), or = to make
each statement true.

19 26 ◯ 29

20 44 ◯ 34

21 26 ◯ 62

Compare using >, <, or =.

22 74 ◯ 77

23 85 ◯ 58

24 126 ◯ 162

25 253 ◯ 235

26 620 ◯ 602

27 825 ◯ 528

28 478 ◯ 488

29 3,294 ◯ 3,924

30 8,925 ◯ 9,825

31 6,706 ◯ 6,760

32 4,106 ◯ 4,016

33 1,997 ◯ 1,799

34 9,172 ◯ 9,712

35 5,296 ◯ 5,269

36 7,684 ◯ 7,684

✓ **Check Understanding**

Explain how to use place value to round multidigit
numbers or compare multidigit numbers.

Round Numbers

Name _____

Discuss and Summarize

Patterns to Millions

Hundred Millions	Ten Millions	Millions	Hundred Thousands	Ten Thousands	Thousands	Hundreds	Tens	Ones
100,000,000	10,000,000	1,000,000	100,000	10,000	1,000	100	10	1
millions			*thousands*			*[ones]*		

The Patterns to Millions chart shows that each digit in the number has a place value name. When we read a number, we do not say the place value name. We say the group name.

We say the word *million* after the digits in the millions group.

We say the word *thousand* after the digits in the thousands group.

We do not say the word *ones* after the digits in the ones group.

To read greater numbers, say each group of digits as if they were in the hundreds, tens, and ones places and then add the special name for that group.

Read Numbers

Use your Whole Number Secret Code cards to make the groups of digits as shown below. Put them in the spaces on the Reading Millions Frame below to read them.

28,374	654,321	92,148	789,321
1,000,000	34,185,726	20,090,870	707,005,009

Reading Millions Frame

0 0 0 0 0 0 0 0 0

millions   *thousands*   *[ones]*

CC SS Content Standards **4.NBT.A.1, 4.NBT.A.2**
Mathematical Practices **MP2, MP3, MP4, MP5, MP6, MP7**

Read and Write Expanded Form

Read and write each number in expanded form.

1 32,568 _30,000 + 2,000 + 500 + 60 + 8_____

2 820,149 _____

3 405,763 _____

4 703,070 _____

Read and write each number in standard form.

5 20,000 + 4,000 + 800 + 10 + 7 _____

6 700,000 + 50,000 + 3,000 + 200 + 90 + 6 _____

7 300,000 + 3,000 + 10 + 9 _____

8 800,000 + 40,000 + 400 + 80 _____

Read and write each number in word form.

9 90,000 + 7,000 + 300 + 20 + 4 _____

10 600,000 + 30,000 + 4,000 + 700 + 30 _____

11 200,000 + 3,000 + 80 + 6 _____

12 500,000 + 20,000 + 400 + 1 _____

Read and write each number in standard form.

13 seventy-eight thousand, one hundred five _____

14 one million _____

15 five hundred sixty-three thousand, fifty-two _____

✔ Check Understanding

Describe the role of a comma when reading and writing multidigit whole numbers.

Compare Greater Numbers

Discuss the problem below.

A stadium hosted both a concert and a sporting event.
The concert had 101,835 people in attendance.
The sporting event had 101,538 people in attendance.
Which event had more people in attendance?
How do you know?

Compare. Write >, <, or = to make each statement true.

1. 12,563 $>$ 11,987
2. 14,615 $<$ 15,651
3. 23,487 $<$ 28,734
4. 83,342 $>$ 80,423
5. 79,131 $>$ 79,113
6. 126,348 ◯ 162,634
7. 705,126 ◯ 705,126
8. 532,834 ◯ 532,843
9. 647,313 ◯ 647,310
10. 198,593 ◯ 98,593
11. 75,621 ◯ 705,126
12. 1,000,000 ◯ 100,000

Greatest Place Value

Round to the nearest ten thousand.

13. 25,987 ___30,000___
14. 13,738 ___10,000___
15. 48,333 ___50,000___
16. 84,562 _____
17. 92,132 _____
18. 99,141 _____

Round to the nearest hundred thousand.

19. 531,987 _____
20. 701,828 _____
21. 670,019 _____
22. 249,845 _____
23. 390,101 _____
24. 999,999 _____

Round to Any Place

Solve.

25 Write a number that changes to 310,000 when it is rounded.
To what place was your number rounded?

_____

26 Write a number that changes to 901,400 when it is rounded.
To what place was your number rounded?

_____

27 Write a number that changes to 800,000 when it is rounded.
To what place was your number rounded?

_____

28 Write a number that changes to 122,000 when it is rounded.
To what place was your number rounded?

_____

29 What is 395,101 rounded to the nearest:

a. ten? _____

b. hundred? _____

c. thousand? _____

d. ten thousand? _____

e. hundred thousand? _____

30 What is 958,069 rounded to the nearest:

a. ten? _____

b. hundred? _____

c. thousand? _____

d. ten thousand? _____

e. hundred thousand? _____

 Check Understanding

Round 465,345 to the ten thousands place. Then compare
the rounded number to the original number using the
symbols >, <, or =.

_____

Name _____

Discuss Different Methods

Discuss how each addition method can be used to add 4-digit numbers.

$$5,879 + 6,754$$

1 New Groups Above Method

Step 1	Step 2	Step 3	Step 4
5,$\overset{1}{8}$79	5,$\overset{11}{8}$79	$\overset{1}{5},\overset{11}{8}$79	$\overset{11}{5},\overset{1}{8}$79
+ 6,754	+ 6,754	+ 6,754	+ 6,754
3	33	633	12,633

2 New Groups Below Method

Step 1	Step 2	Step 3	Step 4
5,879	5,879	5,879	5,879
+ 6,754	+ 6,754	+ 6,754	+ 6,754
$_1$ 3	$_{11}$ 33	$_{111}$ 633	$_{111}$ 12,633

3 Show Subtotals Method (Right-to-Left)

Step 1	Step 2	Step 3	Step 4	Step 5
5,879	5,879	5,879	5,879	5,879
+ 6,754	+ 6,754	+ 6,754	+ 6,754	+ 6,754
13	13	13	13	13
	120	120	120	120
		1,500	1,500	1,500
			11,000	11,000
				+ 11,000
				12,633

PATH to FLUENCY **Practice**

4
```
  908
+ 653
─────
```
1561

5
```
  692
+ 543
─────
```
5235

6
```
  5,362
+ 3,746
───────
```
9108

7
```
  3,786
+ 6,335
───────
```
10521

PATH to FLUENCY Practice (continued)

8 2,782
  + 5,246
  ___8028___

9 6,293
  + 3,862
  ___10,155___

10 3,729
  + 4,541

11 8,196
  + 3,865

12 7,862
  + 2,839

13 2,764
  + 6,648

14 4,825
  + 2,467

15 5,364
  + 4,754

Addition and Money

Think about how to solve this problem.

Carlos is saving money to buy a skateboard. He saved $27
one week and $14 the next week. How much did Carlos
save altogether? _____

Solve each problem.

16 Robyn's grandmother gave her $38 for her birthday and her
uncle gave her $25. How much did Robyn get altogether?

_____

17 A parent-teacher club sold baked goods to raise money
for the school. They collected $268 on Friday and $479 on
Saturday. How much did they collect altogether?

_____

✓ Check Understanding

Explain how you know when to make a new group in addition.

Analyze Different Methods

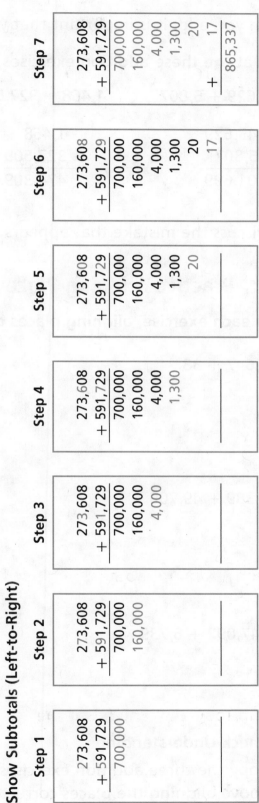

New Groups Above

Step 1
```
  1
  273,608
+ 591,729
        7
```

Step 2
```
  273,608
+ 591,729
       37
```

Step 3
```
  1
  273,608
+ 591,729
      337
```

Step 4
```
  1
  273,608
+ 591,729
    5,337
```

Step 5
```
  1  1
  273,608
+ 591,729
   65,337
```

Step 6
```
  1  1
  273,608
+ 591,729
  865,337
```

New Groups Below

Step 1
```
  273,608
+ 591,729
        7
```

Step 2
```
  273,608
+ 591,729
       37
```

Step 3
```
  273,608
+ 591,729
      337
```

Step 4
```
  273,608
+ 591,729
    5,337
```

Step 5
```
  273,608
+ 591,729
   65,337
```

Step 6
```
  273,608
+ 591,729
  865,337
```

Show Subtotals (Left-to-Right)

Step 1
```
  273,608
+ 591,729
  700,000
```

Step 2
```
  273,608
+ 591,729
  700,000
  160,000
```

Step 3
```
  273,608
+ 591,729
  700,000
  160,000
    4,000
```

Step 4
```
  273,608
+ 591,729
  700,000
  160,000
    4,000
    1,300
```

Step 5
```
  273,608
+ 591,729
  700,000
  160,000
    4,000
    1,300
       20
```

Step 6
```
  273,608
+ 591,729
  700,000
  160,000
    4,000
    1,300
       20
       17
```

Step 7
```
  273,608
+ 591,729
  700,000
  160,000
    4,000
    1,300
       20
+      17
  865,337
```

Find the Mistake

VOCABULARY
digit

When you add, it is important that you add **digits** in like places.

Look at the these addition exercises.

43,629 + 5,807   1,468 + 327,509   470,952 + 4,306

```
    43,629              1,468                470,952
  + 5,807            + 327,509              + 4,306
   1 1                      1 1                1 1
  101,699              474,309               901,552
```

1 Discuss the mistake that appears in all three exercises above.

PATH to FLUENCY **Practice Aligning Places**

Copy each exercise, aligning places correctly. Then add.

2 2,647 + 38   **3** 156 + 83,291

4 4,389 + 49,706   **5** 135,826 + 2,927

6 347,092 + 6,739   **7** 15,231 + 697,084

✓ **Check Understanding**

Copy the three addition exercises in Exercise 1 above aligning the places correctly. Then add to find the correct sums.

Add Greater Numbers

Name

Use Estimation

You can use rounding to estimate a total. Then you can adjust your estimated total to find the exact total.

The best-selling fruits at Joy's Fruit Shack are peaches and bananas. During one month Joy sold 397 peaches and 412 bananas.

$0.60 $0.65

1. *About* how many peaches and bananas did she sell in all?

400 + 400 = 800   iM 8J/1

2. *Exactly* how many peaches and bananas did she sell?

397 412 = 809.   Ill 8J11

Estimate. Then adjust your estimate to find the exact answer.

3. 89 + 28

est = 120
ex = 117

4. 153 + 98

5. 1,297 + 802

6. 1,066 + 45,104

est = 46,206
ex = 46,170

1,100
+45,100
46,200

10 66
+45,104
46,170

Show your work.

16
+30
120

89
+28
117

Solve.

Tomás has $100. He wants to buy a $38 jacket. He also wants to buy a $49 pair of shoes and 2 ties that are on sale, 2 for $8.

7. How can Tomás figure out whether he has enough money for all four items? Does he have enough?

_____

_____

Use Estimation (continued)

Show your work.

Students at Washington Middle School collected 1,598 cans during the first month of their aluminum drive. During the second month of the drive, they collected 2,006 cans.

8 About how many cans did the students collect in all?

_____

9 Exactly how many cans did the students collect in all?

_____

Look for "Easy" Combinations

You can sometimes find number combinations that make it possible to add numbers mentally.

10 Add 243, 274, 252, and 231 vertically.

11 Explain how you can use number combinations to help you add the numbers.

_____

_____

Share Solutions

Find the total. Add mentally if you can.

12	**13**	**14**	**15**	**16**
8	46	35	348	147
4	21	29	516	182
6	+ 64	75	+ 492	108
+ 2		+ 61		+ 165

✓ **Check Understanding**
Find an estimate and the exact total.

37 + 96 + 104 + 64

Estimate: _____   Exact total: _____

Estimation and Mental Math

Name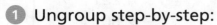

Discuss Ungrouping With Zeros

Look inside the magnifying glass and discuss each ungrouping step.

1 Ungroup step-by-step: *or*   **2** Ungroup all at once:

```
      9  9
   7 10 10 10
   8, 0  0  0
 − 3, 4  9  2
```

```
   7  9  9 10
   8, 0  0  0
 − 3, 4  9  2
```

Decide When to Ungroup

3 Ungroup left-to-right: *or*   **4** Ungroup right-to-left:

```
        15 11
   3  16 12 15
   4, 6  2  5
 − 2, 9  8  7
```

```
        15 11
   3  5  7  15
   4, 6  2  5
 − 2, 9  8  7
```

Other Ungrouping Situations

5 When we have zeros and other digits on the top:

```
   1  16  9 13
   6  10
   2, 7  0  3
 − 1, 9  6  6
```

6 When we have the same digit on the top and bottom:

```
        13 17
   4  14  7 13
   5, 4  8  3
 − 1, 6  8  7
```

Solve and Discuss

Subtract. Show your new groups.

7
```
   8,000
 − 1,691
 ───────
   6,309
```

8
```
   9,462
 − 5,678
 ───────
   3,784
```

9
```
   6,345
 − 2,356
 ───────
   3,989
```

PATH to FLUENCY Practice

Subtract. Show your new groups.

(10)   7,919
      − 3,846

(11)   8,502
      − 3,749

(12)   4,221
      − 2,805

(13)   7,000
      − 572

(14)   4,650
      − 2,793

(15)   4,605
      − 1,711

(16)   3,120
      −   38

(17)   6,082
      −   95

(18)   2,107
      − 428

(19)   1,852
      − 964

(20)   3,692
      − 2,704

(21)   8,715
      − 6,742

(22)   6,000
      − 4,351

(23)   7,400
      − 1,215

(24)   3,583
      − 1,794

Solve.

(25) Jake has 647 pennies in his penny collection album.
The album has space for 1,000 pennies. How many
more pennies can Jake place in his album?

_____

(26) A ship is making an 8,509-mile voyage. So far,
it has sailed 2,957 miles. How many miles of the
voyage remain?

_____

 Check Understanding

Describe how to use ungrouping to subtract from thousands.

Subtract From Thousands

Name _____

Relate Addition to Subtraction

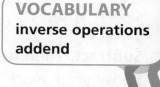

Addition and subtraction are **inverse operations.**
Break-apart drawings help to show inverse relationships.

1 Write a word problem that requires adding 1,310
and 2,057.

_____

_____

_____

_____

2 Write the **addends** and the sum in the break-apart
drawing.

3 Complete the two addition problems represented by
the break-apart drawing.

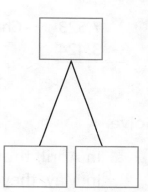

$$\begin{array}{r} 1,310 \\ +\underline{} \\ \hline 3,367 \end{array} \qquad \begin{array}{r} 2,057 \\ +\underline{} \\ \hline \end{array}$$

4 Write a word problem that requires subtracting 1,310
from 3,367.

_____

_____

_____

_____

5 Write two subtraction exercises represented by the
break-apart drawing.

PATH to FLUENCY Practice

**Subtract. Then use addition to check the subtraction.
Show your work.**

6
```
  1,900
−   574
```
Check:

7
```
  1,800
− 1,216
```
Check:

8
```
  5,192
−   341
```
Check:

9
```
  6,350
− 2,460
```
Check:

10
```
  7,523
− 3,424
```
Check:

11
```
  2,000
−   651
```
Check:

Solve.

12 **a.** In April, the zookeepers fed the penguins 4,620 fish.
In May, they fed the penguins 5,068 fish. How many
fish did they feed the penguins altogether?

_____

b. Suppose the head keeper knows the total number
of fish fed to the penguins in April and May, and
knows the penguins were fed 4,620 fish in April.
Show how the keeper can use subtraction to find
the number of fish the penguins were fed in May.
(Use your answer from Part a.)

_____

✓ **Check Understanding**

Describe the relationship between addition and
subtraction. Give examples of related problems.

Subtraction Undoes Addition

Find and Correct Mistakes

Always check your work. Many mistakes can be easily fixed.

What is the mistake in each problem? How can you fix the mistake and find the correct answer?

1 67,308 − 5,497

```
        12
      6 13 10
    6 7 3 0 8
  −   5,4 9 7
    1 2,3 3 8
```

2 134,865 − 5,294

```
    1 3 4,8 6 5
  −     5,2 9 4
    1 3 1,6 3 1
```

_____
_____
_____
_____
_____

Check Subtraction by "Adding Up"

"Add up" to find any places where there is a subtraction mistake. Discuss how each mistake might have been made and correct the subtraction if necessary.

3
```
    163,406
  −  84,357
     79,159
```

4
```
    526,741
  − 139,268
    413,473
```

5
```
  1,000,000
  − 300,128
    600,872
```

6
```
  5,472,639
  − 2,375,841
    3,096,798
```

7 Write and solve a subtraction problem with numbers in the hundred thousands.

Estimate Differences

You can use estimation to decide if an answer is reasonable.

Dan did this subtraction: 8,196 − 5,980. His answer was 3,816. Discuss how using estimation can help you decide if his answer is correct.

Decide whether each answer is reasonable. Show your estimate.

8 4,914 − 949 = 3,065

_____

_____

9 52,022 − 29,571 = 22,451

_____

_____

Solve.   *Show your work.*

10 Bob has 3,226 marbles in his collection. Mia has 1,867 marbles. Bob says he has 2,359 more than Mia. Is Bob's answer reasonable? Show your estimate.

_____

11 Two towns have populations of 24,990 and 12,205. Gretchen says the difference is 12,785. Is Gretchen's answer reasonable? Show your estimate.

_____

12 Estimate to decide if the answer is reasonable. If it is not reasonable, describe the mistake and find the correct answer.

$$\begin{array}{r} 805{,}716 \\ -\ 290{,}905 \\ \hline 614{,}811 \end{array}$$

_____

_____

_____

Check Understanding

Describe how subtracting and ungrouping with greater numbers is similar to subtracting and ungrouping with lesser numbers.

Subtract Greater Numbers

Discuss the Steps of the Problem

Sometimes you will need to work through more than one step to solve a problem. The steps can be shown in one or more equations.

1 In the morning, 19 students were working on a science project. In the afternoon, 3 students left and 7 more students came to work on the project. How many students were working on the project at the end of the day?

_____

2 Solve the problem again by finishing Anita's and Chad's methods. Then discuss what is alike and what is different about each method.

Anita's Method	Chad's Method
Write an equation for each step.	**Write an equation for the whole problem.**
Find the total number of students who worked on the project.	Let $n=$ the number of students working on the project at the end of the day.
$$19 + 7 = \underline{\quad}$$	Students who left in the afternoon. Students who arrived in the afternoon.
Subtract the number of students who left in the afternoon.	$$19 - \underline{\quad} + \underline{\quad} = n$$
$$26 - 3 = \underline{\quad}$$	$$\underline{\quad} = n$$

3 Solve. Discuss the steps you used.

A team is scheduled to play 12 games. Of those games, 7 will be played at home. The other games are away games. How many fewer away games than home games will be played?

_____

_____

Share Solutions

Solve each problem.

Show your work.

4 The school library has 288 science books. Altogether the library has 618 science and animal books. How many fewer science books than animal books does the library have?

_____

5 Olivia's stamp collection consists of 442 stamps. There are 131 animal stamps and 107 famous people stamps in her collection. How many of Olivia's stamps are not of animals or famous people?

_____

(PATH to FLUENCY) ## Practice Multidigit Addition and Subtraction

6
$$985 - 792$$

7
$$2{,}931 + 8{,}563$$

8
$$4{,}201 + 9{,}979$$

9
$$98{,}309 - 48{,}659$$

10
$$78{,}196 - 14{,}587$$

11
$$21{,}682 + 95{,}436$$

12
$$373{,}095 + 185{,}543$$

13
$$709{,}032 - 239{,}125$$

14
$$540{,}721 + 375{,}699$$

✓ **Check Understanding**

Describe how to solve two-step problems.

Practice Addition and Subtraction

Name _____

Discuss Problem Types

Think of different types of problems for each exercise.
Write an equation for the problem then solve it.

1 $a + 278 = 747$

747
/ \
a 278

2 $b - 346 = 587$

b
/ \
346   587

3

933
/ \
c 346

4

747

e	469

_____   _____   _____   _____

_____   _____   _____   _____

PATH to FLUENCY Share Solutions

Write an equation for the problem then solve it.
Make a math drawing if you need to.

Show your work.

5 Of 800,000 species of insects, about 560,000 undergo complete metamorphosis. How many species do not undergo complete metamorphosis?

_____

_____

6 The Great Pyramid of Giza has about 2,000,000 stone blocks. A replica has 1,900,000 fewer blocks. How many blocks are in the replica?

_____

_____

7 Last year 439,508 people visited the science museum. This is 46,739 fewer visitors than this year. How many people visited the science museum this year?

_____

_____

© Houghton Mifflin Harcourt Publishing Company

PATH to FLUENCY **Share Solutions (continued)**

Show your work.

8 At the end of a baseball game, there were 35,602 people in the stadium. There were 37,614 people in the stadium at the beginning of the game. How many people left before the game ended?

_____

_____

9 This year Pinnacle Publishing printed 64,924 more books than Premier Publishing. If Pinnacle printed 231,069 books, how many books did Premier print?

_____

_____

10 Mary drove her car 2,483 miles during a road trip. Now she has 86,445 miles on her car. How many miles did her car have before her trip?

_____

_____

11 The Yellow River in China is 5,465 kilometers long. It is 4,295 kilometers longer than the Elbe River in Europe. How long is the Elbe River?

_____

_____

12 A bridge is 1,595 feet long. Each cable holding up the bridge is 1,983 feet longer than the bridge itself. How long is each cable?

_____

_____

Problem Solving With Greater Numbers

Name _____

Subtraction and Money

Sondra had $140 to spend on new clothes for school. She bought a shirt for $21. You can use a model to help you find out how much money she has left.

Sondra had _____ left.

Solve each problem. Use money if you need to.

Show your work.

13 Jason had $30. He gave $18 to his brother. How much money does Jason have left?

_____

14 Elana's coach had some money to spend on softball equipment. She spent $76 on bases. She has $174 left. How much did she have to start?

_____

15 The school science club raised $325. After buying equipment for an experiment they had $168 left. How much did they spend?

_____

16 Amy's family has a budget of $850 for buying new furniture. They buy a couch for $575. How much is left in their furniture budget?

_____

Problem Solving With Greater Numbers **37**

Determine Reasonable Answers

Solve each problem. Check your answers using inverse operations.

17. Mrs. Washington has $265. She wants to buy shoes for $67 and dresses for $184. Does she have enough money? Explain your answer. _____

18. Terrell wants to run at least 105 miles during the month. He ran a total of 87 miles during the first 3 weeks of the month. If he runs 25 miles in the fourth week, will he make his goal? Explain. _____

What's the Error?

Dear Math Students,

My friend is taking a trip to Antarctica. He gave me $112 to buy him some clothes. I tried to buy a parka and two pairs of wool socks, but the clerk said I didn't have enough money. I added the cost like this:

$98 + $12 = $110

Can you help me figure out what I did wrong?

Your friend,
Puzzled Penguin

Bill's Outdoor Wear

Pair of wool socks	$12
Hat	$15
Mittens	$10
Parka	$98

19. Write a response to Puzzled Penguin.

_____

_____

✓ Check Understanding

If Puzzled Penguin wanted to buy a parka and a hat, what would the total be? _____ Does Puzzled Penguin have enough money? _____

Problem Solving With Greater Numbers

Name

Make a Bar Graph

Bridges are structures that are built to get over obstacles like water, a valley, or roads. Bridges can be made of concrete, steel, or even tree roots. Engineers and designers do a lot of math to be sure a bridge will stand up to its use and the forces of nature that affect it.

Lengths of Bridges		
Bridge	**Length Over Water (ft)**	
Manchac Swamp Bridge, U.S.A.	121,440	
Hangzhou Bay Bridge, China	117,057	
Lake Pontchartrain Causeway, U.S.A.	125,664	
Jiaozhou Bay Bridge, China	139,392	

1 Use the data in the table above to make a bar graph.

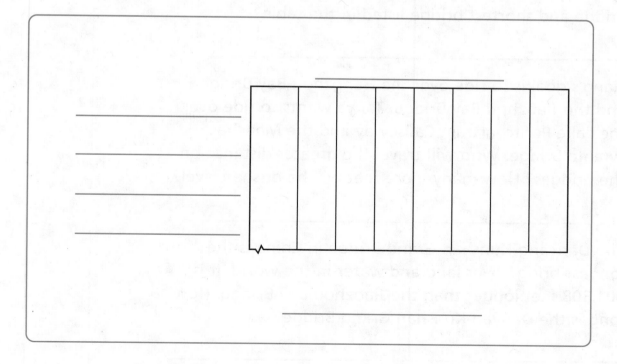

Add and Subtract Greater Numbers

The Lake Pontchartrain Causeway is composed of two parallel bridges crossing Lake Pontchartrain in Louisiana. It is the longest bridge in the United States.

For Problems 2–5, use the data in the table on page 39.

Show your work.

2 How much longer is the Lake Pontchartrain Causeway than the Hangzhou Bay Bridge?

_____

3 What is the difference in length between the longest bridge and shortest bridge listed in the table?

_____

4 Liang's goal is to ride over the Hangzhou Bay Bridge and the Jiaozhou Bay Bridge. Tanya wants to ride over the Lake Pontchartrain Causeway and the Manchac Swamp Bridge. Who will travel the greater distance on the bridges? How many more feet will he or she travel?

_____

5 The Danyang-Kunshan Grand Bridge in China is the longest bridge over land and water in the world. It is 401,308 feet longer than the Jiaozhou Bay Bridge. How long is the Danyan-Kunshan Grand Bridge?

_____

Focus on Mathematical Practices

1 Anthony's family drives 659 miles from Miami to Atlanta. Then they drive another 247 miles to Nashville. How far does Anthony's family drive in all? Show your work.

2 A scientist measures 3,470 milliliters of water into a beaker. She pours 2,518 milliliters of the water in a solution. If the beaker can hold 5,000 milliliters, how much water is needed to fill the beaker? Show your work. Then show a way to check your answer.

3 Fill in the blank to show the number of hundreds.

4,500 = _____ hundreds

Explain how you know.

4 A mining truck is loaded with 147,265 kilograms of
dirt. Another 129,416 kilograms of dirt is added. What
is the total mass of the dirt in the mining truck? Show
your work.

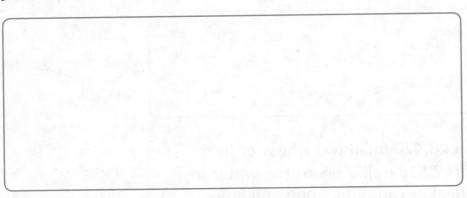

5 The downtown location of Mike's Bikes earned $179,456
last year. The store's riverside location earned $145,690.
The store with the greater earnings gets an award.
Which store gets the award? Show your work.

6 Select another form of 65,042. Mark all that apply.

(A) 6 + 5 + 0 + 4 + 2

(B) sixty-five thousand, forty-two

(C) 60,000 + 5,000 + 40 + 2

(D) six hundred fifty, forty-two

7 For numbers 7a–7e, choose Yes or No to tell if the number is rounded to the nearest thousand.

7a. 234,566
235,000 ○ Yes ○ No

7b. 7,893
7,900 ○ Yes ○ No

7c. 64,498
65,000 ○ Yes ○ No

7d. 958,075
958,000 ○ Yes ○ No

7e. 49,826
50,000 ○ Yes ○ No

8 For numbers 8a–8e, choose True or False to describe the statement.

8a. 34,639 > 34,369 ○ True ○ False

8b. 2,709 = 2,790 ○ True ○ False

8c. 480,920 > 480,902 ○ True ○ False

8d. 259 < 261 ○ True ○ False

8e. 6,924 < 6,299 ○ True ○ False

9 Make a place value drawing for 1,534.

10 For numbers 10a–10e, write 685,203 rounded to the nearest place value.

10a. ten _____

10b. hundred _____

10c. thousand _____

10d. ten thousand _____

10e. hundred thousand _____

11 For numbers 11a–11d, find the sum or difference.

11a.   4,379
     + 3,284

11c.   389,416
     + 237,825

11b.   57,340
     − 26,817

11d.   648,939
     − 584,172

12 There were 2,683 books sold at a bookstore this year. There were 1,317 more books sold last year. How many books were sold last year? Write an equation for the problem then solve it. Show your work.

13 Wren added the numbers 1,376 and 6,275.

Part A

Write the addends and the sum in the break-apart drawing. Then complete the two addition problems represented by the break-apart drawing.

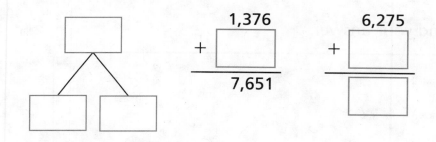

Part B

Write a word problem that requires subtracting 1,376 from 7,651.

14 Last week there were two soccer games. There were
3,982 people at the first soccer game. There were 1,886
fewer people at the second soccer game than at the
first soccer game.

Part A

How many people attended the soccer games last
week? Show your work.

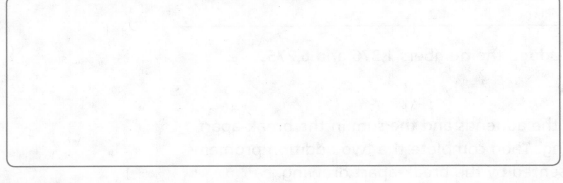

Part B

Explain how you found your answer.

15 Order the numbers from least to greatest by writing a
number in each box.

6,857	5,768	5,687	6,578	5,678

least   greatest

Track Blog Traffic

James used a tool to see how much traffic his blog was getting.

Blog Traffic

Month	Unique Users	Number of Unique Users (Rounded)
January	389	400
February	3,725	4,000
March	41,692	40,000

1 James is reporting his blog's growing popularity to a journalist. She asks James how many more unique users visited the blog in February than in January. Should James find the difference using the actual number of unique users or the rounded number of unique users? Explain your answer.

_____

_____

_____

_____

2 On March 3, James's blog was featured in an online gaming journal. How many more unique users visited James's website in March than in February?

_____

3 Look at the *Number of Unique Users (Rounded)* column in the table. Describe a pattern.

_____

4 Is it realistic to expect this pattern to continue? Explain why or why not. Use addition or subtraction patterns to support your answer.

_____

_____

_____

_____

One of the unique users is a computer at a school library. In any given month, anywhere from 250 to 1,200 individual students use this library computer.

5 Consider what you know about the computer in the school's library. Suppose you wanted to include the number of individual students who visited James's blog from that computer. How might the data change?

Complete the table below including your new data.

Blog Traffic

Month	Unique Users + students	Number of Users (Rounded)
January		
February		
March		

6 Explain why you chose the number that you entered for January's data.

_____

_____

_____

7 Explain why you chose the number that you entered for February's data.

_____

_____

_____

8 Explain how you changed the data in March, after James's blog was featured in an online gaming journal.

_____

_____

_____

Dear Family:

In this unit, your child will be learning about the common multiplication method that most adults know. However, they will also explore ways to draw multiplication. *Math Expressions* uses area of rectangles to show multiplication.

	30	+	7
20	20 × 30 = 600		20 × 7 = 140
+			
4	4 × 30 = 120		4 × 7 = 28

Area Method:

$$20 \times 30 = 600$$
$$20 \times 7 = 140$$
$$4 \times 30 = 120$$
$$\underline{4 \times 7 = 28}$$
$$\text{Total} = 888$$

Shortcut Method:

$$\overset{1}{}\overset{2}{}$$
$$37$$
$$\underline{\times \, 24}$$
$$148$$
$$\underline{74}$$
$$888$$

Area drawings help all students see multiplication. They also help students remember what numbers they need to multiply and what numbers make up the total.

Your child will also learn to find products involving single-digit numbers, tens, and hundreds by factoring the tens or hundreds. For example,

$$200 \times 30 = 2 \times 100 \times 3 \times 10$$
$$= 2 \times 3 \times 100 \times 10$$
$$= 6 \times 1{,}000 = 6{,}000$$

By observing the zeros patterns in products like these, your child will learn to do such multiplications mentally.

If your child is still not confident with single-digit multiplication and division, we urge you to set aside a few minutes every night for multiplication and division practice. In a few more weeks, the class will be doing multidigit division, so it is very important that your child be both fast and accurate with basic multiplication and division.

If you need practice materials, please contact me.

Sincerely,
Your child's teacher

CC SS Unit 2 addresses the following standards from the Common Core State Standards for Mathematics: **4.OA.A.3, 4.NBT.A.1, 4.NBT.A.2, 4.NBT.A.3, 4.NBT.B.5, 4.MD.A.2,** and all Mathematical Practices.

Estimada familia:

En esta unidad, su niño estará aprendiendo el método de multiplicación común que la mayoría de los adultos conoce. Sin embargo, también explorará maneras de dibujar la multiplicación. Para mostrar la multiplicación, *Math Expressions* usa el método del área del rectángulo.

	30	+	7
20	$20 \times 30 = 600$		$20 \times 7 = 140$
+			
4	$4 \times 30 = 120$		$4 \times 7 = 28$

Método del área

$20 \times 30 = 600$
$20 \times 7 = 140$
$4 \times 30 = 120$
$4 \times 7 = 28$
Total $= 888$

Método más corto

$$\begin{array}{r} \overset{1}{}\overset{2}{} \\ 37 \\ \times\ 24 \\ \hline 148 \\ 74 \\ \hline 888 \end{array}$$

Los dibujos de área ayudan a los estudiantes a visualizar la multiplicación. También los ayuda a recordar cuáles números tienen que multiplicar y cuáles números forman el total.

Su niño también aprenderá a hallar productos relacionados con números de un solo dígito, con decenas y con centenas, factorizando las decenas o las centenas. Por ejemplo:

$$200 \times 30 = 2 \times 100 \times 3 \times 10$$
$$= 2 \times 3 \times 100 \times 10$$
$$= 6 \times 1,000 = 6,000$$

Al observar los patrones de ceros en productos como estos, su niño aprenderá a hacer dichas multiplicaciones mentalmente.

Si su niño todavía no domina la multiplicación y la división con números de un solo dígito, le sugerimos que dedique algunos minutos todas las noches para practicar la multiplicación y la división. Dentro de pocas semanas, la clase hará divisiones con números de varios dígitos, por eso es muy importante que su niño haga las operaciones básicas de multiplicación y de división de manera rápida y exacta.

Si necesita materiales para practicar, comuníquese conmigo.

Atentamente,
El maestro de su niño

En la Unidad 2 se aplican los siguientes estándares de los Estándares estatales comunes de matemáticas: **4.OA.A.3, 4.NBT.A.1, 4.NBT.A.2, 4.NBT.A.3, 4.NBT.B.5, 4.MD.A.2 y todos los de** Prácticas matemáticas.

area

estimate

array

factor

Distributive Property

partial product

A number close to an exact amount or to find about how many or how much.

The number of square units that cover a figure.

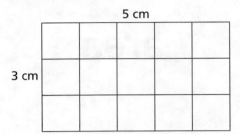

One of two or more numbers multiplied to find a product.

Example:

$$4 \times 5 = 20$$

factor   factor   product

An arrangement of objects, symbols, or numbers in rows and columns.

The product of the ones, or tens, or hundreds, and so on in multidigit multiplication.

Example:

```
   24
 ×  9
   36  ←  partial product (9 × 4)
  180  ←  partial product (9 × 20)
  216
```

You can multiply a sum by a number, or multiply each addend by the number and add the products; the result is the same.

Example:

$$3 \times (2 + 4) = (3 \times 2) + (3 \times 4)$$

$$3 \times 6 = \quad 6 \quad + \quad 12$$

$$18 \quad = \qquad 18$$

product

rounding

**square unit
(unit²)**

The answer to a multiplication problem.

Example:

$9 \times 7 = 63$

↑

product

Finding the nearest ten, hundred, thousand, or some other place value. The usual rounding rule is to round up if the next digit to the right is 5 or more and round down if the next digit to the right is less than 5.

Examples:

463 rounded to the nearest ten is 460.
463 rounded to the nearest hundred is 500.

A unit of area equal to the area of a square with one-unit sides.

Name _____

Model a Product of Ones

The number of unit squares in an **array** of connected unit squares is the **area** of the rectangle formed by the squares. We sometimes just show the measurement of length and width.

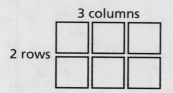 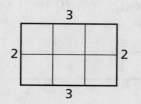 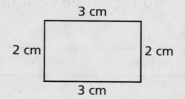

You can draw a rectangle for any multiplication. In the real world, we use multiplication for finding both sizes of arrays and areas of figures.

A 2 × 3 rectangle has 6 unit squares inside, so 2 × 3 = 6.

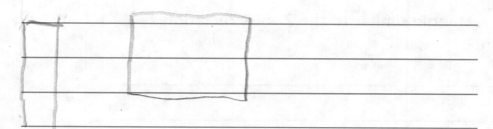

1 On your MathBoard, draw a 3 × 2 rectangle. How is the 3 × 2 rectangle similar to the 2 × 3 rectangle? How is it different?

_____

2 How do the areas of the 2 × 3 and 3 × 2 rectangles compare?

_____

_____

_____

Factor the Tens to Multiply Ones and Tens

VOCABULARY
square units

This 2 × 30 rectangle contains 2 groups of 30 unit squares.

$$
\begin{array}{c}
30 \\
\begin{array}{|c|}
\hline
1 \times 30 = 30 \\
\hline
1 \times 30 = 30 \\
\hline
\end{array} \\
30
\end{array}
$$

This 2 × 30 rectangle contains 3 groups of 20 unit squares.

30 = 10 + 10 + 10

| $2 \times 10 = 20$ | $2 \times 10 = 20$ | $2 \times 10 = 20$ |

10 + 10 + 10

This 2 × 30 rectangle contains 6 groups of 10 unit squares, so its area is 60 **square units**.

30 = 10 + 10 + 10

| $1 \times 10 = 10$ | $1 \times 10 = 10$ | $1 \times 10 = 10$ |
| $1 \times 10 = 10$ | $1 \times 10 = 10$ | $1 \times 10 = 10$ |

10 + 10 + 10

3 How can we show this numerically? Complete the steps.

$$2 \times 30 = (2 \times 1) \times (\underline{3} \times 10)$$
$$= (\underline{2} \times \underline{3}) \times (1 \times 10)$$
$$= \underline{6} \times 10 = 60$$

4 How is a 30 × 2 rectangle similar to the 2 × 30 rectangle? How is it different?

_____

_____

_____

_____

✓ **Check Understanding**

Draw a model to represent 4 × 20. Then show how to find 4 × 20 by factoring the tens.

Arrays and Area Models

Name _____

Use Place Value to Multiply

You have learned about the Base Ten Pattern in place value. This model shows how place value and multiplication are connected.

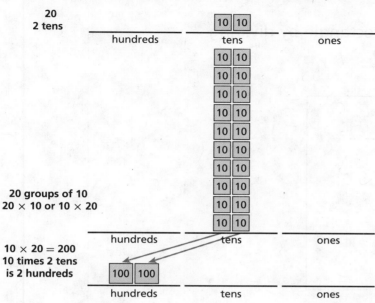

20
2 tens

hundreds — tens | 10 | 10 — ones

20 groups of 10
20 × 10 or 10 × 20

hundreds — tens — ones

10 × 20 = 200
10 times 2 tens
is 2 hundreds

hundreds | 100 | 100 — tens — ones

You can use properties to show the relationship between place value and multiplication.

Associative Property	$10 \times 20 = 10 \times (2 \times 10)$
	$= (10 \times 2) \times 10$
Commutative Property	$= (2 \times 10) \times 10$
Associative Property	$= 2 \times (10 \times 10)$
	$= 2 \times 100$
	$= 200$

1 Ten times any number of tens gives you that number of hundreds. Complete the steps to show 10 times 5 tens.

$$10 \times 50 = 10 \times (\; \underline{5} \; \times \; \underline{10} \;)$$
$$= (10 \times \underline{5}\;) \times \underline{10}$$
$$= (\; \underline{5} \; \times 10) \times \underline{100}$$
$$= \underline{5} \times (10 \times \underline{10}\;)$$
$$= \underline{5} \times \underline{100}$$
$$= \underline{500}$$

Model a Product of Tens

Olivia wants to tile the top of a table. The table is 20 inches by 30 inches.

2 Find the area of this 20 × 30 rectangle by dividing it into 10-by-10 squares of 100.

20×30 =

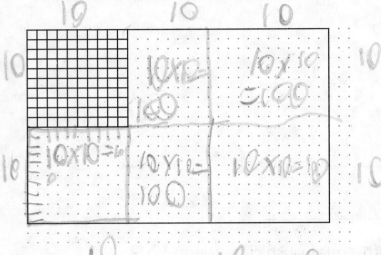

10

10 10 10

10 10 10

3 Each tile is a 1-inch square. How many tiles does Olivia need to cover the tabletop? 600

4 Each box of tiles contains 100 tiles. How many boxes of tiles does Olivia need to buy? 6

Factor the Tens

5 Show your work in Exercise 2 numerically.

20 × 30 = (____2____ × 10) × (____3____ × 10)

= (____2____ × ____3____) × (10 × 10)

= ____6____ × 100 = 600

6 Is it true that 20 × 30 = 30 × 20? Explain how you know.

_____

✓ Check Understanding

Explain how to find 40 × 20 by factoring the tens.

Connect Place Value and Multiplication

Name ______________________

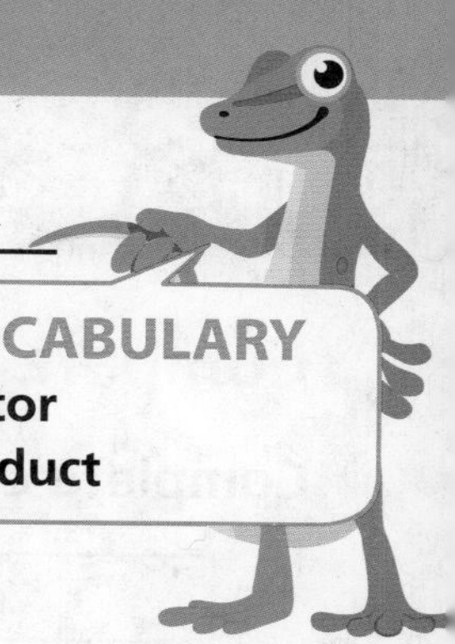

VOCABULARY
factor
product

Look for Patterns

Multiplying greater numbers in your head is easier when you learn patterns of multiplication with tens.

Start with column A and look for the patterns used to get the expressions in each column. Complete the table.

Table 1

	A	B	C	D
	2×3	$2 \times 1 \times 3 \times 1$	6×1	6
1	2×30	$2 \times 1 \times 3 \times 10$	6×10	60
2	20×30	$2 \times 10 \times 3 \times 10$	6x100	600

3 How are the expressions in column B different from the expressions in column A?

Factor each number/digit and mutiply by the place value

4 In column C, we see that each expression can be written as a number times a place value. Which of these **factors** gives more information about the size of the **product**?

____

5 Why is 6 the first digit of the products in column D?

____

6 Why are there different numbers of zeros in the products in column D?

____

Compare Tables

Complete each table.

Table 2			
A	**B**	**C**	**D**
6 × 3	6 × 1 × 3 × 1	18 × 1	18
7 6 × 30	6 × 1 × 3 × 10	18 × 10	180
8 60 × 30	6 × 10 × 3 × 10	18×100	1,800

Table 3			
A	**B**	**C**	**D**
5 × 8	5 × 1 × 8 × 1	40 × 1	40
9 5 × 80	5 × 1 × 8 × 10	40 × 10	400
10 50 × 80	5×10×8×10	40×100	4,000

11 Why do the products in Table 2 have more digits than the products in Table 1 on page 57?

_____

_____

12 Why are there more zeros in the products in Table 3 than the products in Table 2?

_____

_____

✔ **Check Understanding**
Complete.

$50 × 60 = ($ __5__ $× 10) × (6 ×$ __10__ $) =$ __30__ $× 100 =$ __3000__

Mental Math and Multiplication

Name _____

Explore the Area Model

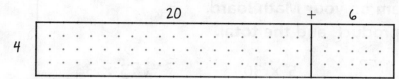

1 How many square units of area are there in the tens part of the drawing?

_____

2 What multiplication equation gives the area of the tens part of the drawing? Write this equation in its rectangle.

_____

3 How many square units of area are there in the ones part?

_____

4 What multiplication equation gives the area of the ones part? Write this equation in its rectangle.

_____

5 What is the total of the two areas?

_____

6 How do you know that 104 is the correct product of 4×26?

_____

7 Read Problems A and B.

A. Al's photo album has 26 pages. Each page has 4 photos. How many photos are in Al's album?

B. Nick took 4 photos. Henri took 26 photos. How many more photos did Henri take than Nick?

Which problem could you solve using the multiplication you just did? Explain why.

_____

_____

© Houghton Mifflin Harcourt Publishing Company

Use Rectangles to Multiply

**Draw a rectangle for each problem on your MathBoard.
Find the tens product, the ones product, and the total.**

8 3 × 28

_____

_____

_____

9 3 × 29

_____

_____

_____

10 5 × 30

_____

_____

_____

11 5 × 36

_____

_____

_____

12 4 × 38

_____

_____

_____

13 8 × 38

_____

_____

_____

14 4 × 28

_____

_____

_____

15 5 × 28

_____

_____

_____

Solve each problem.

Show your work.

16 Maria's father planted 12 rows of tomatoes in his garden. Each row had 6 plants. How many tomato plants were in Maria's father's garden?

_____

17 A library subscribes to 67 magazines. Each month the library receives 3 copies of each magazine. How many magazines does the library receive each month?

_____

18 Complete this word problem. Then solve it.

_____ has _____ boxes of _____.

There are _____ _____ in each box.

How many _____ does _____

have altogether? _____

Model One-Digit by Two-Digit Multiplication

Name _____

Multiply One-Digit Dollar Amounts by Two-Digit Numbers

You can use your skills for multiplying a one-digit number by a two-digit number to multiply one-digit dollar amounts by two-digit numbers.

Find the exact cost. Give your answer in dollars.

Show your work.

19 A small package of construction paper costs $2. If someone is purchasing 24 packages, how much will it cost?

_____

20 A box lunch can be purchased for $3. How much will 83 lunches cost?

_____

21 A movie ticket costs $8 per person. If 61 people go to the 10:00 A.M. show, how much money does the theater collect for that show?

_____

22 A round-trip train ticket costs $4 per child. If 58 fourth graders take a class trip to the city on the train, how much will the train tickets cost altogether?

_____

23 Admission to the planetarium costs $8 per student. If a group of 72 students takes a trip to the planetarium, how much will their tickets cost altogether?

_____

24 Sara earns $9 per hour as a cashier. How much does she earn in a 40-hour week?

_____

Multiply Two-Digit Dollar Amounts by One-Digit Numbers

You can use your skills for multiplying a one-digit number by a two-digit number to multiply one-digit numbers by two-digit dollar amounts.

Find the exact cost. Give your answer in dollars.

Show your work.

25 A tricycle costs $53. If 2 tricycles are purchased, how much will the total cost be?

_____

26 A store sells used video games for $14 each. If someone buys 7 of them, how much will they cost altogether?

_____

27 An aquarium admission fee is $23 per person. If 4 friends go to the aquarium, how much will their tickets cost altogether?

_____

28 A car rental costs $72 per day. How much will it cost to rent a car for 3 days?

_____

29 A bus ticket costs $87. How much will 6 tickets cost?

_____

30 Jorge earns $99 each week. He goes on vacation in 9 weeks. How much will he earn before his vacation?

_____

✓ **Check Understanding**

Draw an area model to represent Problem 28. Then explain how to use the model to find the product.

Model One-Digit by Two-Digit Multiplication

Name _____

Estimate Products

VOCABULARY
estimate
rounding

It is easier to **estimate** the product of a two-digit number and a one-digit number when you think about the two multiples of ten close to the two-digit number. This is shown in the drawings below.

1. In each drawing, find the rectangles that represent 4×70 and 4×60. These rectangles "frame" the rectangles for 4×68 and 4×63. Find the values of 4×70 and 4×60.

   $4 \times 70 =$ ___280___ $4 \times 60 =$ ___240___

2. Look at the rectangle that represents 4×68. Is 4×68 closer to 4×60 or to 4×70? So is 4×68 closer to 240 or 280?

   _____

3. Look at the rectangle that represents 4×63. Is 4×63 closer to 4×60 or to 4×70? Is 4×63 closer to 240 or 280?

   _____

4. Explain how to use **rounding** to estimate the product of a one-digit number and a two-digit number.

   _____

   _____

   _____

CC SS Content Standards **4.NBT.A.3, 4.NBT.B.5**
Mathematical Practices **MP1, MP2, MP3, MP6**

Practice Estimation

Explain how rounding and estimation could help solve these problems.

5 Keesha's school has 185 fourth-grade students. The library has 28 tables with 6 chairs at each table. Can all of the fourth graders sit in the library at one time? How do you know?

_____

_____

_____

6 Ameena is printing the class newsletter. There are 8 pages in the newsletter, and she needs 74 copies. Each package of paper contains 90 sheets. How many packages of paper does she need to print the newsletter?

_____

_____

_____

_____

Estimate each product. Then solve to check your estimate.

7 3×52 $\underline{3 \times 50 = 150}$
156

8 7×48 $\underline{7 \times 50 = 350}$
336

9 9×27 $\underline{9 \times 30 = 270}$
243

10 8×34 $\underline{8 \times 30 = 240}$
272

✓ **Check Understanding**

Explain how you can use rounding to estimate 3×57.

Name _____

Use the Place Value Sections Method

You can use an area model to demonstrate the Place Value Sections Method. This strategy is used below for multiplying a one-digit number by a two-digit number.

Complete the steps.

27 =	20	+ 7
5	5 × 20 = 100	5 × 7 = 35

5
$$\begin{array}{r} 100 \\ + 35 \\ \hline 135 \end{array}$$

Use the Place Value Sections Method to solve the problem. Complete the steps.

1 The fourth-grade class is participating in a walk-a-thon. Each student will walk 8 laps around the track. There are 92 fourth-grade students. How many laps will the fourth-grade class walk?

_____

92 =	90	+ 2
8	___ × ___ = ___	___ × ___ = ___

8
$$\begin{array}{r} 720 \\ + 16 \\ \hline 736 \end{array}$$

Draw an area model and use the Place Value Sections Method to solve the problem.

2 A football coach is ordering 3 shirts for each football player. There are 54 players in the football program. How many shirts does the coach need to order for the entire program?

_____

Use the Expanded Notation Method

You can also use an area model to show how to use the
Expanded Notation Method.

Use the Expanded Notation Method to solve each problem.

3

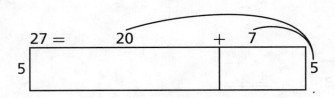

27 = 20 + 7

5   5

$$27 = 20 + 7$$
$$\times\ 5 = \quad\quad 5$$
$$5 \times 29 = 199$$
$$5 \times 7 = 35$$
$$135$$

4 A farm stand sold 4 bushels of apples in one day.
Each bushel of apples weighs 42 pounds. How many
pounds of apples did the farm stand sell?

_____

42 = 40 + 2

4   4

$$42 = 40 + 2$$
$$4 =\quad\quad 4$$
$$4 \times 40 = 160$$
$$4 \times 2 = 8$$
$$168$$

5 A marina needs to replace the boards on their pier.
The pier is 7 feet by 39 feet. What is the area of
the pier?

_____

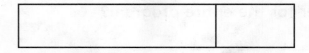

✓ **Check Understanding**

Do you prefer to use the Place Value Sections Method or
the Expanded Notation Method? Explain your answer.

      Use Place Value to Multiply

Name _____

Model the Distributive Property

You have used area models to help you multiply. You can use the area model to find 3 × 74 by writing 74 in expanded form and using the **Distributive Property** to find **partial products**. After you find all the partial products, you can add them together to find the actual product of 3 × 74.

Complete each exercise.

1 Write 74 in expanded form.

3 × 74 = 3 (_____ + _____)

2 Use the Distributive Property.

3 × 74 = (_____ × _____) + (_____ × _____)

The area models below show the steps to find the solution to 3 × 74.

STEP 1   74 =   70   +   4
3 | 3 × 70 = 210 | | 3
Multiply the tens.

(3 × 70) = _____

STEP 2   74 =   70   +   4
3 | | 3 × 4 = 12 | 3
Multiply the ones.

(3 × 4) = _____

STEP 3   74 =   70   +   4
3 | 3 × 70 = 210 | 3 × 4 = 12 | 3
Add the   210
partial products.   + 12
                    _____

3 What is the actual product of 3 × 74? _____

Use the Algebraic Notation Method to Multiply

Another numerical multiplication method that can be represented by an area model is the Algebraic Notation Method. This method also decomposes the two-digit factor into tens and ones and then uses the Distributive Property.

Use the Algebraic Notation Method to solve each problem. Complete the steps.

4 8 · 62

$62 = \underline{60} \quad + \underline{2}$

8

$8 \cdot 62 = \underline{8} \cdot (\underline{60} + \underline{2})$
$= 480 + 16$
$= 496$

5 2 · 97

$97 = \underline{90} \quad + \underline{7}$

2

$2 \cdot 97 = \underline{2} \cdot (\underline{90} + \underline{7})$
$= 180 + 14$
$= 194$

Draw an area model and use the Algebraic Notation Method to solve the problem.

6 There are 9 members on the school's golf team. Each golfer hit a bucket of 68 golf balls at the driving range. How many golf balls did the entire team hit?

 9 x 68

✓ Check Understanding

Draw an area model and use it to explain how to use the Algebraic Notation Method to find 4 × 86.

Algebraic Notation Method

Name _____

Numerical Multiplication Methods

You have used the area model to help you multiply. In this lesson, you will compare the numerical multiplication methods that are related to this area model.

Place Value Sections Method

```
37 =              30              +     7
   ┌──────────────────────────────┬─────────────┐
 4 │        4 × 30 = 120          │ 4 × 7 = 28  │ 4
   └──────────────────────────────┴─────────────┘
```

```
   120
 + 28
 ─────
   148
```

Expanded Notation Method

```
37 =              30              +     7
   ┌──────────────────────────────┬─────────────┐
 4 │                              │             │ 4
   └──────────────────────────────┴─────────────┘
```

```
37 =  30 + 7
×  4 =      4
─────────────
4 × 30 = 120
4 ×  7 =  28
─────────────
         148
```

Algebraic Notation Method

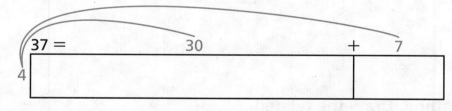

```
37 =           30            +    7
 ┌─────────────────────────────┬──────────┐
4│                             │          │
 └─────────────────────────────┴──────────┘
```

```
4 × 37 = 4 × (30 + 7)
       = 120 + 28
       = 148
```

Connect the Multiplication Methods

Refer to the examples above.

1 What two values are added together to give the answer in all three methods?

_____

2 What is different about the three methods?

_____

Practice Different Methods

Fill in the blanks in the following solutions.

3 4×86

Expanded Notation

$$86 = \underline{\qquad} + 6$$

$$\times \quad 4 = \underline{\qquad}$$

$$4 \times \underline{\qquad} = \underline{\qquad}$$

$$\underline{\qquad} \times 6 = 24$$

$$\underline{\qquad}$$

Algebraic Notation

$$4 \cdot 86 = \underline{\qquad} \cdot (80 + 6)$$

$$= 320 + \underline{\qquad}$$

$$= \underline{\qquad}$$

4 4×68

Expanded Notation

$$\underline{\qquad} = 60 + 8$$

$$\times \quad 4 = \underline{\qquad}$$

$$4 \times \underline{\qquad} = \underline{\qquad}$$

$$\underline{\qquad} \times 8 = 32$$

$$\underline{\qquad}$$

Algebraic Notation

$$4 \cdot 68 = 4 \cdot (\underline{\qquad} + \underline{\qquad})$$

$$= 240 + \underline{\qquad}$$

$$= \underline{\qquad}$$

Solve using a numerical method. Draw the related area model.

5 $5 \times 64 = \underline{\qquad}$

6 $6 \times 72 = \underline{\qquad}$

✓ **Check Understanding**

For Exercise 6, which numerical method did you use?

_____

Explain why you chose that method.

Compare Methods of One-Digit by Two-Digit Multiplication

Compare Multiplication Methods

Compare these methods for solving 9 × 28.

Method A	**Method B**	**Method C**	**Method D**
$28 = 20 + 8$	$28 = 20 + 8$	28	28
$\times\ 9 =\qquad 9$	$\times\ 9 =\qquad 9$	$\times\quad 9$	$\times\quad 9$
$9 \times 20 = 180$	$\qquad\quad 180$	$\qquad 180$	$\qquad 72$
$9 \times 8 =\ 72$	$\qquad\quad\ 72$	$\qquad\ 72$	$\qquad 180$
$\qquad\qquad 252$	$\qquad\quad 252$	$\qquad 252$	$\qquad 252$

1 How are all the methods similar? List at least two similarities.

_____

_____

_____

2 How are the methods different? List at least three differences.

_____

_____

_____

_____

Discuss how the recording methods below show the partial products in different ways.

Show Partial Products Method	**Show New Groups Method**
$\quad 28$	$\quad 28$
$\times\quad 9$	$\times\quad 9$
$\quad 72 \quad 9 \times 8$	$\ ^{1\ 7}$
$+\ 180 \quad 9 \times 2 \text{ tens}$	$\underline{\quad 82}$
	$\quad 252$

© Houghton Mifflin Harcourt Publishing Company

Discuss the Shortcut Method

The steps for the Shortcut Method are shown below.

Shortcut Method with New Groups Above			Shortcut Method with New Groups Below		
Method E:	**Step 1**	**Step 2**	**Method F:**	**Step 1**	**Step 2**
	$\overset{7}{2}8$	$\overset{7}{2}8$		28	28
	$\times\ 9$	$\times\ 9$		$\times\ 9$	$\times\ 9$
	2	252		$\overset{7}{}2$	$\overset{7}{2}52$

③ Where are the products 180 and 72 from Methods A–D?

_____

_____

_____

_____

Practice Multiplication

Solve using any method. Sketch a rectangle if necessary.

④ 63
 $\times\ 5$
 315

⑤ 39
 $\times\ 8$
 312

⑥ 98
 $\times\ 2$
 196

⑦ 86
 $\times\ 4$

⑧ 25
 $\times\ 7$

⑨ 47
 $\times\ 9$

⑩ 76
 $\times\ 3$

⑪ 54
 $\times\ 6$

✓ Check Understanding

Choose any method shown in this lesson. Explain step-by-step how to use that method to solve 4×37.

Discuss Different Methods

Name _____

Use Rectangles to Multiply Hundreds

You can use a model to show multiplication with hundreds. Study this model to see how we can multiply 7 × 300.

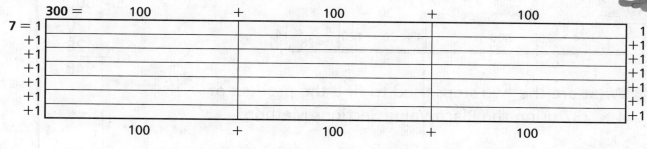

$$7 \times 300 = 7 \times (3 \times 100) = (7 \times 3) \times 100$$
$$= 21 \times 100$$
$$= 2,100$$

1 How many hundreds are represented in each column of the model?

_____

2 How does knowing that 7 × 3 = 21 help you find 7 × 300?

_____

_____

3 What property of multiplication is used in the equation, 7 × (3 × 100) = (7 × 3) × 100?

_____

4 Sketch a model of 6 × 400. Be ready to explain your model.

Compare the Three Methods

You can use the **Place Value Sections Method** to multiply a one-digit number by a three-digit number.

237 =	200	+	30	+ 7	
4	4 × 200 = 800		4 × 30 = 120	4 × 7 = 28	4

```
  800
  120
+  28
-----
  948
```

5 What are the two steps used to find the product of 4 × 237 using the Place Value Sections Method?

_____

The **Expanded Notation Method** uses the same steps as the Place Value Sections Method.

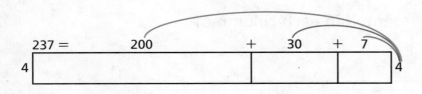

$$237 = 200 + 30 + 7$$
$$\times \ 4 = \qquad\qquad\qquad 4$$
$$4 \times 200 = 800$$
$$4 \times 30 = 120$$
$$4 \times 7 = \ \ 28$$
$$948$$

6 What is the last step in the Expanded Notation Method and the Place Value Sections Method?

_____

The **Algebraic Notation Method** uses expanded form just like the other two methods. Even though the steps look different, they are the same as in the other methods.

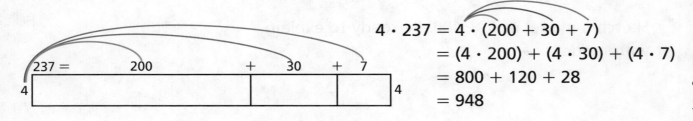

$$4 \cdot 237 = 4 \cdot (200 + 30 + 7)$$
$$= (4 \cdot 200) + (4 \cdot 30) + (4 \cdot 7)$$
$$= 800 + 120 + 28$$
$$= 948$$

7 What is the first step in all three methods?

_____

One-Digit by Three-Digit Multiplication

Name

Practice Multiplication

Solve using any method. Show your work.
Draw an area model if necessary.

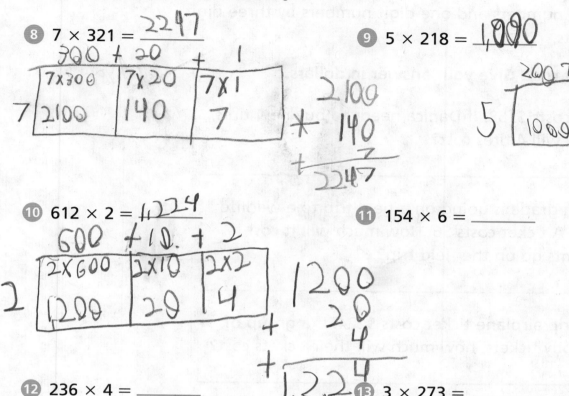

(8) 7 × 321 = 2247

700 + 20 + 1

7×700	7×20	7×1
7| 2100 | 140 | 7 |

2100
× 140
+   7
  2247

(9) 5 × 218 = 1,090

200 + 10 + 8

200	10	8
5| 1000 | 50 | 40 |

1000
+ 50
+ 40
1090

(10) 612 × 2 = 1224

600 + 10 + 2

2×600	2×10	2×2
2| 1200 | 20 | 4 |

1200
20
4
+ 1224

(11) 154 × 6 = _____

(12) 236 × 4 = _____

(13) 3 × 273 = _____

(14) 482 × 9 = _____

(15) 8 × 615 = _____

9 [   ]

One-Digit by Three-Digit Multiplication **77**

Multiplication With Dollar Amounts

You can use your skills for multiplying a one-digit number by a three-digit number to multiply one-digit dollar amounts by three-digit numbers and one-digit numbers by three-digit dollar amounts.

Find the exact cost. Give your answer in dollars.

Show your work.

16 A car tire costs $158. If Danica needs to buy new tires, how much will 4 tires cost?

_____

17 The fourth grade is going on a field trip to a wildlife sanctuary. A ticket costs $6. How much will it cost if 127 students go on the field trip?

_____

18 A round-trip airplane ticket costs $224. If a group of 5 people buy tickets, how much will their tickets cost?

_____

19 A bookstore orders 325 copies of a book at $7 each. How much does the store pay for the books?

_____

20 During the summer, Joe makes $115 each week mowing lawns. How much will Joe make in 9 weeks?

_____

21 A ticket to the school talent show costs $8. There are 540 seats. If all the seats are filled, how much money does the school collect for that show?

_____

✓ Check Understanding

Find the product of a 3-digit number and a 1-digit number using any method. Explain your method.

Name _____

Discuss Problems With Too Much Information

A word problem may sometimes include more information than you need. Read the following problem and then answer each question.

Mrs. Sanchez is putting a border around her garden. Her garden is a rectangle with dimensions 12 feet by 18 feet. The border material costs $3.00 per foot. How many feet of border material is needed?

1 Identify any extra numerical information. Why isn't this information needed?

_____

_____

2 Solve the problem. _____

Solve each problem. Cross out information that is not needed.

Show your work.

3 ~~Judy downloaded an album for $15.~~ The album has 13 songs. Each song is 3 minutes long. How long will it take to listen to the whole album?

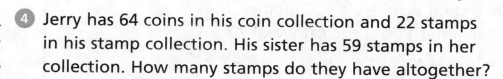

3×13

$$\begin{array}{r} 13 \\ \times\ 3 \\ \hline 39 \text{ minutes} \end{array}$$

4 Jerry has 64 coins in his coin collection and 22 stamps in his stamp collection. His sister has 59 stamps in her collection. How many stamps do they have altogether?

5 Adrian has been playing the piano for 3 years. He practices 20 minutes a day. He is preparing for a recital that is 9 days away. How many minutes of practice will he complete before the recital?

_____

Discuss Problems With Too Little Information

When solving problems in real life, you need to determine what information is needed to solve the problem. Read the following problem and then answer each question.

The campers and staff of a day camp are going to an amusement park on a bus. Each bus holds 26 people. How many buses will be needed?

6 Do you have enough information to solve this problem? What additional information do you need?

_____

_____

Determine if the problem can be solved. If it cannot be solved, tell what information is missing. If it can be solved, solve it.

7 Richard is saving $5 a week to buy a bike. When will he have enough money?

How much the bike is

8 Natalie wants to find out how much her cat weighs. She picks him up and steps on the scale. Together, they weigh 94 pounds. How much does the cat weigh?

How much nautlie weys

9 Phyllis wants to make 8 potholders. She needs 36 loops for each potholder. How many loops does she need?

_____

10 For one of the problems that could not be solved, rewrite it so it can be solved and then solve it.

_____

_____

Multistep Word Problems

Name _____

Discuss Problems With Hidden Questions

Mrs. Norton bought 2 packages of white cheese with 8 slices in each pack. She bought 3 packages of yellow cheese with 16 slices in each pack. How many more slices of yellow cheese than white cheese did she buy?

11 What do you need to find?

_____

_____

12 What are the hidden questions?

_____

_____

13 Answer the hidden questions to solve the problem.

How many slices of white cheese? $2 \times 8 =$ _____

How many slices of yellow cheese? $3 \times 16 =$ _____

How many more slices of yellow cheese? $48 - 16 =$ _____

Read the problem. Then answer the questions.

Show your work.

Maurice has 6 boxes of markers. June has 5 boxes of markers. Each box contains 8 markers. How many markers do Maurice and June have altogether?

14 Write the hidden questions.

_____

_____

15 Solve the problem.

_____

_____

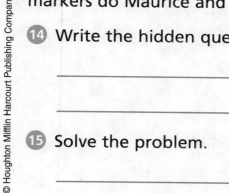

Mixed Problem Solving

Show your work.

16 Mr. Collins counts 54 cartons and 5 boxes of paper clips. Each carton contains 8 boxes. A box of paper clips costs $2. How many boxes of paper clips does he have?

_____

17 Ms. Wu has 5 cartons of black ink and 4 cartons of color ink. Each carton contains 48 cartridges. How many ink cartridges are there in all?

_____

What's the Error?

Dear Math Students,

My school is collecting cans for a food drive. There are 608 students in the school. A can of soup costs about $2. Each student will bring in 3 cans. I wrote this multiplication to find the number of cans the school will collect in all.

Is my answer correct? Can you help me?

Your friend,
Puzzled Penguin

$$\begin{array}{r} \overset{2}{608} \\ \times\ \ 3 \\ \hline 1,864 \end{array}$$

18 Write a response to Puzzled Penguin.

_____

_____

 Check Understanding

Does Puzzled Penguin's problem have too much information or a hidden question?

_____

Write the information that is extra or the question that is hidden.

_____

© Houghton Mifflin Harcourt Publishing Company

Multistep Word Problems

Name _____

Compare Models

A coin-collecting book holds 24 coins on a page. There are 37 pages in the book. How many coins can the book hold? The models below all show the solution to 24 × 37.

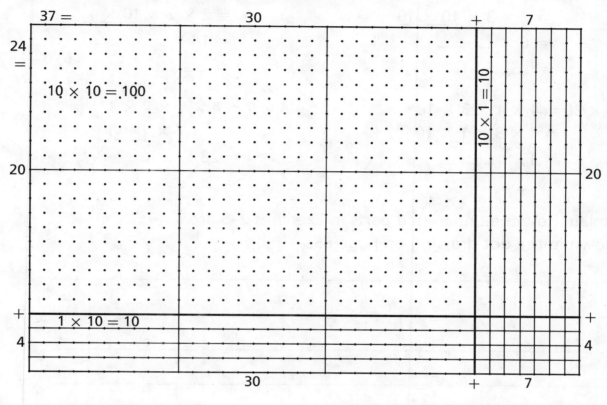

Area Model Sketch

Place Value Sections Method

$$20 \times 30 = \mathbf{600}$$
$$20 \times 7 = \mathbf{140}$$
$$4 \times 30 = \mathbf{120}$$
$$\underline{4 \times 7 = \mathbf{28}}$$

1. Describe how each model shows 6 hundreds, 14 tens, 12 tens, and 28 ones.

CC SS Content Standards **4.NBT.A.2, 4.NBT.B.5**
Mathematical Practices **MP3, MP4, MP5, MP6**

Investigate Products in the Sketch

Complete each equation.

2 $20 \times 30 = 2 \times 10 \times 3 \times 10$
$\qquad = 2 \times 3 \times \underline{10 \times 10}$
$\qquad = 6 \times \underline{\hspace{1cm}}$
$\qquad = \underline{\hspace{1cm}}$

3 $20 \times 7 = 2 \times 10 \times 7 \times 1$
$\qquad = 2 \times 7 \times \underline{10 \times 1}$
$\qquad = 14 \times \underline{\hspace{1cm}}$
$\qquad = \underline{\hspace{1cm}}$

4 $4 \times 30 = 4 \times 1 \times 3 \times 10$
$\qquad = 4 \times 3 \times \underline{1 \times 10}$
$\qquad = 12 \times \underline{\hspace{1cm}}$
$\qquad = \underline{\hspace{1cm}}$

5 $4 \times 7 = 4 \times 1 \times 7 \times 1$
$\qquad = 4 \times 7 \times \underline{1 \times 1}$
$\qquad = 28 \times \underline{\hspace{1cm}}$
$\qquad = \underline{\hspace{1cm}}$

6 Explain how the underlined parts in Exercises 2–5 are shown in the dot drawing on page 85.

_____

_____

_____

_____

7 Find 24×37 by adding the products in Exercises 2–5.

_____

Practice and Discuss Modeling

Use your MathBoard to sketch an area drawing for each exercise. Then find the product.

8 36×58 _____

9 28×42 _____

10 63×27 _____

11 26×57 _____

12 86×35 _____

13 38×65 _____

✓**Check Understanding**

Write 4 multiplications you could use to find 25×31.

____ × ____ 　 ____ × ____ 　 ____ × ____ 　 ____ × ____

Two-Digit by Two-Digit Multiplication

Compare Multiplication Methods

Each area model is the same. Study how these three methods of recording 43 × 67 are related to the area models.

Place Value Sections Method

67 =	60	7	
40	40 × 60 = 2,400	40 × 7 = 280	40
3	3 × 60 = 180	3 × 7 = 21	3
	60	7	

$$40 \times 60 = 2,400$$
$$40 \times 7 = 280$$
$$3 \times 60 = 180$$
$$3 \times 7 = 21$$
$$\overline{2,881}$$

Expanded Notation Method

67 =	60	7	
40	40 × 60 = 2,400	40 × 7 = 280	40
3	3 × 60 = 180	3 × 7 = 21	3
	60	7	

$$67 = 60 + 7$$
$$\times\ 43 = 40 + 3$$
$$40 \times 60 = 2,400$$
$$40 \times 7 = 280$$
$$3 \times 60 = 180$$
$$3 \times 7 = 21$$
$$2,881$$

Algebraic Notation Method

67 =	60	7	
40	40 × 60 = 2,400	40 × 7 = 280	40
3	3 × 60 = 180	3 × 7 = 21	3
	60	7	

$$43 \cdot 67 = (40 + 3) \cdot (60 + 7)$$
$$= 2,400 + 280 + 180 + 21$$
$$= 2,881$$

1. What is alike about all the three methods?

Other Ways to Record Multiplication

Discuss how the recording methods below show the partial products in different ways.

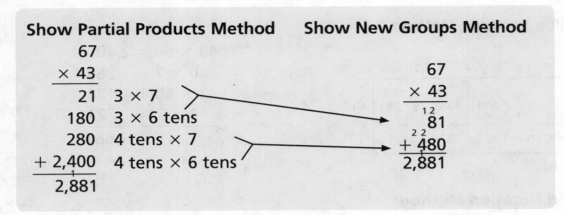

Show Partial Products Method

```
      67
    × 43
      21   3 × 7
     180   3 × 6 tens
     280   4 tens × 7
  + 2,400  4 tens × 6 tens
     ¹
   2,881
```

Show New Groups Method

```
        67
      × 43
       ¹²
        81
       ²²
    + 480
    2,881
```

The Shortcut Method

New Groups Above

Step 1	Step 2	Step 3	Step 4	Step 5
² 67 × 43 1	² 67 × 43 201	²² 67 × 43 201 8	²² 67 × 43 201 268	²² 67 × 43 201 + 268 2,881

New Groups Below

```
      67
    × 43
     ²²
     201
   + 268
   2,881
```

Discuss how this area drawing relates to the Shortcut Method.

```
                    67
        ┌──────────────────────────┐
   40   │   40 × 67 = 2,680         │
        ├──────────────────────────┤
   +    │                          │
   3    │   3 × 67 = 201           │
        └──────────────────────────┘
```

✓ **Check Understanding**

Explain how to use any method to multiply 36 × 74.

Different Methods for Two-Digit Multiplication

Estimate Products

Products of two-digit factors can be estimated by rounding each factor to the nearest ten.

Estimate and then solve.

1 28 × 74

30×70

2100; 2072

2 84 × 27

_____

3 93 × 57

_____

4 87 × 54

_____

5 38 × 62

_____

6 65 × 39

_____

7 26 × 43

30×40

1200; 1118

_____

8 59 × 96

_____

9 53 × 74

_____

10 Write a multiplication word problem. Estimate the product and then solve.

_____

_____

_____

_____

_____

11 Would using an estimate be problematic in the situation you wrote for Exercise 10? Explain why or why not.

_____

_____

_____

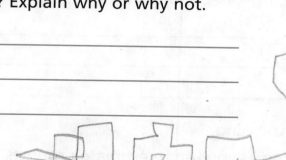

© Houghton Mifflin Harcourt Publishing Company

What's the Error?

Dear Math Students,

My friends and I are going to build 42 flower boxes. The building plans say each box needs 13 nails. I rounded to estimate how many nails we'll need. Since $40 \times 10 = 400$, I bought a box of 400 nails.

My friends say we won't have enough nails. Did I make a mistake? Can you help me estimate how many nails we need?

Your friend,
Puzzled Penguin

12 Write a response to Puzzle Penguin.

_____

_____

_____

Estimate and then solve. Explain whether the estimate is problematic in each situation.

13 Sally hires a dog sitter for her 18-day trip. A dog sitter charges $14 per day. How much money will Sally need to pay the dog sitter?

_____

_____

14 An artist draws a plan for a mosaic pattern that has 21 rows of tiles with 47 tiles in each row. How many tiles does the artist need to buy?

_____

_____

_____

✓ **Check Understanding**
Describe strategies you use to estimate products.

Check Products of Two-Digit Numbers

Name ________________________________

Practice Multiplication Methods

1 Multiply 38 × 59.

Shortened Expanded Notation Method

$$\begin{array}{r} 38 \\ \times\ 59 \\ \hline \end{array}$$

Shortcut Method

$$\begin{array}{r} 38 \\ \times\ 59 \\ \hline \end{array}$$

Solve using any method and show your work. Check your work with estimation.

2 43 × 22 946

	20 + 2	
40 +	40x20 800	40x2 80
3	3x20 60	6

800 + 80 + 60 + 6 = 946

3 25 × 25 625

$$\begin{array}{r} 25 \\ \times\ 25 \\ \hline 125 \\ 500 \\ \hline 625 \end{array}$$

4 31 × 62 1922

$$\begin{array}{r} 62 \\ +1860 \\ \hline 1922 \end{array}$$

5 54 × 72 ________

6 81 × 33 2459

$$\begin{array}{r} 81 \\ \times\ 33 \\ \hline 43 \\ 2416 \\ \hline 2459 \end{array}$$

7 49 × 62 3038

$$\begin{array}{r} 49 \\ \times\ 62 \\ \hline 98 \\ +2940 \\ \hline 3038 \end{array}$$

© Houghton Mifflin Harcourt Publishing Company

Practice Multiplication

With practice, you will be able to solve a multiplication problem using fewer written steps.

Solve.

Show your work.

8 Between his ninth and tenth birthdays, Jimmy read 1 book each week. There are 52 weeks in a year. If each book had about 95 pages, about how many pages did he read during the year?

_____

9 Sam's father built a stone wall in their backyard. The wall was 14 stones high and 79 stones long. How many stones did he use to build the wall?

_____

10 Balloon Bonanza sells party balloons in packages of 25 balloons. There are 48 packages in the store. How many balloons are in 48 packages?

_____

11 Brian is buying T-shirts for the marching band. He knows that at parades the band forms 24 rows. Each row has 13 students. If T-shirts come in boxes of 100, how many boxes of T-shirts should Brian buy?

_____

✓ **Check Understanding**

Find the product of 35×56 using any method.

_____

Practice Multiplication

Use Rectangles to Multiply Thousands

You can use a model to multiply greater numbers.
Notice that each of the smaller rectangles in this model
represents one thousand. Each of the columns represents
seven one-thousands or 7,000.

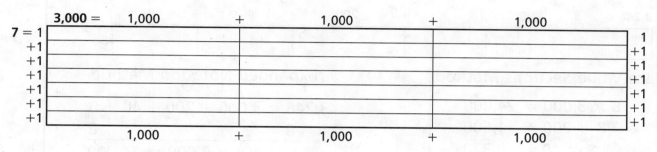

$$7 \times 3{,}000 = 7 \times (3 \times 1{,}000) = (7 \times 3) \times 1{,}000$$
$$= 21 \times 1{,}000$$
$$= 21{,}000$$

1 While multiplying by thousands, how many zeros can
you expect in the product?

_____

2 How does thinking of 3,000 as 3 × 1,000 help you to
multiply 7 × 3,000?

_____

_____

_____

_____

3 Draw a model for 4 × 8,000. Then find the product.

Compare Multiplication Methods

You can use the multiplication methods you have learned to multiply a one-digit number by a four-digit number.

Find 8 × 3,248.

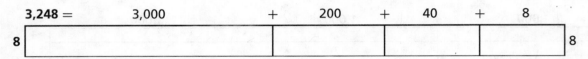

3,248 =	3,000	+	200	+	40	+	8	
8								8

Place Value Sections Method

$$8 \times 3,000 = 24,000$$
$$8 \times 200 = 1,600$$
$$8 \times 40 = 320$$
$$8 \times 8 = 64$$
$$\overline{25,984}$$

Expanded Notation Method

$$3,248 = 3,000 + 200 + 40 + 8$$
$$\times \quad 8 = \qquad\qquad\qquad 8$$
$$\overline{}$$
$$8 \times 3,000 = 24,000$$
$$8 \times 200 = 1,600$$
$$8 \times 40 = 320$$
$$8 \times 8 = 64$$
$$\overline{25,984}$$

Algebraic Notation Method

$$8 \times 3,248 = 8 \times (3,000 + 200 + 40 + 8)$$
$$= (8 \times 3,000) + (8 \times 200) + (8 \times 40) + (8 \times 8)$$
$$= 24,000 + 1,600 + 320 + 64$$
$$= 25,984$$

Make a rectangle drawing for each problem on your MathBoard. Then solve the problem using the method of your choice.

④ $3 \times 8,153 = $ _____

⑤ $4 \times 2,961 = $ _____

⑥ $6 \times 5,287 = $ _____

⑦ $7 \times 1,733 = $ _____

✓ Check Understanding

Draw a model for $9 \times 5,432$. Then find the product using the method of your choice.

Multiply One-Digit and Four-Digit Numbers

Name _____

Compare Methods of Multiplication

Look at the drawing and the six numerical solutions for 4 × 2,237.

2,237 =	2,000	+	200	+	30	+	7

4 [_____ | _____ | _____ | ____] 4

Method A	**Method B**	**Method C**	**Method D**	**Method E**	**Method F**
2,237 = 2,000 + 200 + 30 + 7	2,237 = 2,000 + 200 + 30 + 7	2,237	2,237	¹ ²2,237	2,237
× 4 = 4	× 4 = 4	× 4	× 4	× 4	× 4
4 × 2,000 = 8,000	8,000	8,000	28	8,948	+ ¹ ²
4 × 200 = 800	800	800	120		8,948
4 × 30 = 120	120	120	800		
4 × 7 = 28	28	28	8,000		
8,948	8,948	8,948	8,948		

1 How are the solutions similar? List at least two ways.

_____

_____

_____

2 How are the solutions different? List at least three comparisons between methods.

_____

_____

_____

_____

_____

3 How do Methods A–D relate to the drawing? List at least two ways.

_____

_____

_____

Analyze the Shortcut Method

Look at this breakdown of solution steps for Method E and Method F.

Method E			
Step 1	**Step 2**	**Step 3**	**Step 4**
$\overset{2}{2{,}237}$	$\overset{1\,2}{2{,}237}$	$\overset{1\,2}{2{,}237}$	$\overset{1\,2}{2{,}237}$
$\times \quad 4$	$\times \quad 4$	$\times \quad 4$	$\times \quad 4$
8	48	948	$8{,}948$

Method F			
Step 1	**Step 2**	**Step 3**	**Step 4**
$2{,}237$	$2{,}237$	$2{,}237$	$2{,}237$
$\times \underset{2}{\quad 4}$	$\times \underset{1\,2}{\quad 4}$	$\times \underset{1\,2}{\quad 4}$	$\times \underset{1\,2}{\quad 4}$
8	48	948	$8{,}948$

④ Describe what happens in Step 1.

_____

_____

_____

⑤ Describe what happens in Step 2.

_____

_____

_____

⑥ Describe what happens in Step 3.

_____

_____

_____

⑦ Describe what happens in Step 4.

_____

_____

_____

Round and Estimate With Thousands and Hundreds

You can use what you know about rounding and multiplication with thousands to estimate the product of $4 \times 3{,}692$.

8 Find the product if you round up: $4 \times 4{,}000 =$ _____

9 Find the product if you round down: $4 \times 3{,}000 =$ _____

10 Which one of the two estimates will be closer to the actual solution? Why?

_____

11 Calculate the actual solution. _____

12 Explain why neither estimate is very close to the actual solution.

_____

_____

13 What would be the estimate if you added 4×600 to $4 \times 3{,}000$; $(4 \times 3{,}000) + (4 \times 600)$? _____

14 What would be the estimate if you added 4×700 to $4 \times 3{,}000$; $(4 \times 3{,}000) + (4 \times 700)$? _____

15 Estimate $4 \times 7{,}821$ by rounding $7{,}821$ to the nearest thousand.

_____

16 Find the actual product. _____

17 Find a better estimate for $4 \times 7{,}821$. Show your work.

_____

_____

Round, estimate, and fix the estimate as needed.

18 $6 \times 3{,}095$

_____

_____

19 $7 \times 2{,}784$

_____

_____

Estimate Products

Solve and then estimate to check if your answer is reasonable. Show your estimate.

20 $5 \times 3{,}487 =$ _____

_____

_____

21 $7 \times 8{,}894 =$ _____

_____

_____

22 $4 \times 7{,}812 =$ _____

_____

_____

23 $3 \times 4{,}109 =$ _____

_____

_____

What's the Error?

Dear Math Students,

My school collected 2,468 empty cartons of milk today. If the school collects about the same number of cartons each day for 5 days, I estimated that the school will collect 17,500 cartons.

$$(5 \times 3{,}000) + (5 \times 500) = 17{,}500$$

Can you help me decide if this is a reasonable estimate?

Your friend,
Puzzled Penguin

24 Write a response to Puzzled Penguin.

_____

_____

_____

✔ Check Understanding

Multiply $6 \times 5{,}283$ using the Shortcut Method. _____
Round and estimate to check your work.

_____

Use the Shortcut Method

Name

Practice Mixed Multiplication

Solve using any method and show your work. Check your work with estimation.

1 35×9

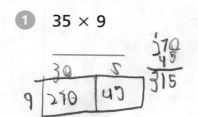

2 56×17

952

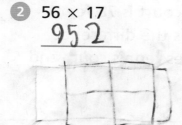

3 228×2

456

4   23
    $\times\ 7$

5   77
    $\times\ 9$

6   59
    $\times\ 3$

7   92
    $\times\ 84$

8   49
    $\times\ 12$

9   61
    $\times\ 36$

10   459
    $\times\ \ 4$

11   588
    $\times\ \ 6$

12   216
    $\times\ 7$

13   3,473
    $\times\ \ \ \ 5$

14   1,156
    $\times\ \ \ \ 8$

15   2,937
    $\times\ \ \ \ 3$

© Houghton Mifflin Harcourt Publishing Company

Practice With Word Problems

Solve using any method and show your work.
Check your work with estimation.

Show your work.

16 A doubles tennis court is 78 feet long and 36 feet wide. A singles tennis court is 78 feet long and 27 feet wide. What is the difference between the areas of a doubles tennis court and a singles tennis court?

_____

17 A movie complex has 8 theaters. Each theater has 287 seats. There are 13 people who work at the theater. How many seats are there altogether?

_____

18 Jenny goes to a 55-minute-long dance class 3 days each week. There are 9 weeks until the class recital. How many minutes of dance class are there until the recital?

_____

19 Alex is shopping for school clothes. He buys 4 shirts for $12 each. He also buys 3 pairs of shorts for $17 each. How much does Alex spend on school clothes in all?

_____

20 Casey draws a rectangular array that is 1,167 units long and 7 units wide. What is the area of Casey's array?

_____

✔ **Check Understanding**

Multiply 4 × 6,689 using any method. _____
Check your work with estimation.

Practice Multiplying

Name _____

Math and Games

This is a game called *Big City Building*. The goal of the game is to design and build a successful city within a budget. To win the game, the city must have all of the features of a real-life city such as apartments, schools, parks, and shops, so its residents will be happy.

1. Each city in *Big City Building* requires a fire station, a police station, and a post office. These each cost $2,657 in taxes per year to maintain. How much does it cost to maintain the fire station, the police station, and the post office building for one year?

   _____

2. In *Big City Building*, the roads are standard two-lane roads. The total width of the road is 9 meters. If each block is 82 meters long, what is the area of the road of one city block in square meters?

   _____

Content Standards 4.NBT.B.5, 4.MD.A.2
Mathematical Practices MP1, MP2, MP3, MP4, MP5, MP6

Big City Building

The table shows the cost of different features on the *Big City Building* game. Below is Scott's design, so far, for his city in *Big City Building*.

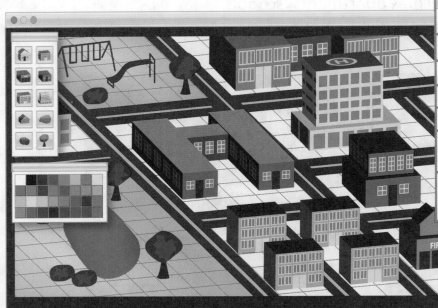

Item	Cost
Tree	$83 per tree
Shrub	$54 per shrub
Lake	$198 per square unit
Road	$288 per square unit
Apartment building	$9,179 per building
Any other building	$892 per square unit

Currently, Scott has $156,324 in *Big City Building* money to create his city.

3 Scott buys 42 trees to put in the park. The trees cost $83 each. How much money does Scott pay for the trees?

_____

4 Each apartment building contains 59 apartment units. Scott has 4 apartment buildings in his city. How many apartment units does Scott's city have?

_____

5 If Scott's city is 27 units long and 19 units wide, what is the area of Scott's city in square units?

_____

Focus on Mathematical Practices

1 Use the numbers on the tiles to complete the steps to find
20 × 40 by factoring the tens.

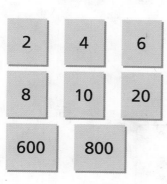

2	4	6
8	10	20
600	800	

20 × 40 = (2 × 10) × (40 × 10)

= (2 × 4) × (10 × 10)

= 8 × 100

= 800

2 Select the expression that is equivalent to 36 × 25.
Mark all that apply.

(A) 30 × 6 + 20 × 5

(B) (30 × 20) + (30 × 5) + (6 × 20) + (6 × 5)

(C) (5 × 6) + (5 × 3 tens) + (2 tens × 6) + (2 tens × 3 tens)

(D) 30 × (20 + 5) + 6 × (20 + 5)

(E) 30 + 15 + 12 + 6

3 There are 24 pencils in a box. If there are 90 boxes,
how many pencils are there?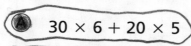

2160 pencils

4 A clown bought 18 bags of round balloons with 20 balloons
in each bag. He bought 26 bags of long balloons with
35 balloons in each bag. How many more long balloons
are there than round balloons? Show your work.

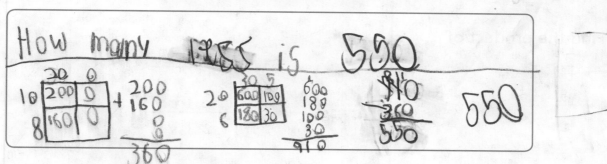

5 Draw an area model for 7 × 682.

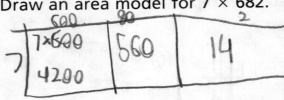

Explain how you used the model to find the product.

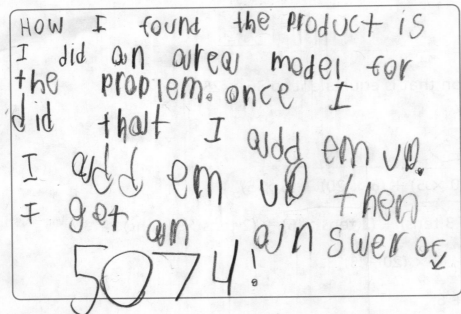

> HOW I found the PRoduct is
> I did an area model for
> the problem. once I
> did that I add em uρ
> I add em uρ then
> I get an answer of
> 5074!

6 For Exercises 6a–6d, choose Yes or No to tell whether the equation is true.

6a. 8 × 4 = 32   ● Yes   ○ No

6b. 8 × 400 = 32,000   ● Yes   ○ No

6c. 80 × 40 = 3,200   ○ Yes   ● No

6d. 8 × 4,000 = 32,000   ● Yes   ○ No

7 Find the product of 4 × 52.

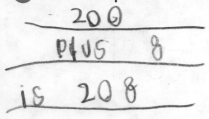

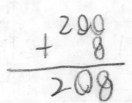

8 Use the numbers on the tiles to complete the area model for 29 × 48.

(handwritten worked column: 800 + 360 160 72 1382)

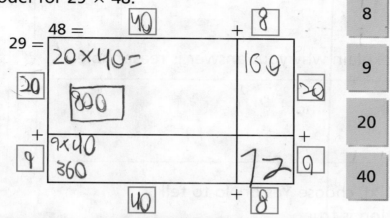

(tiles: 8, 9, 20, 40)

(area model: 48 = 40 + 8; 29 = 20 + 9)
20 × 40 = 800 | 160
9 × 40 360 | 72

Show how to use the area model and expanded notation to find 29 × 48.

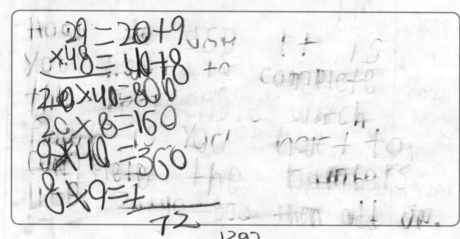

(handwritten work:
29 = 20 + 9
× 48 = 40 + 8
20 × 40 = 800
20 × 8 = 160
9 × 40 = 360
8 × 9 = 72
1392)

9 Estimate 15 × 34 by rounding each number to the nearest ten.

20 × 30 = 600

600

10 For Exercises 10a–10d, choose True or False to describe the statement.

10a. 8 × 93 is greater than 8 × 90.   ● True   ○ False

10b. An estimate of 8 × 93 is 2,700.   ○ True   ● False

10c. 8 × 93 = (8 × 9) + (8 × 3)   ● True   ○ False

10d. 8 × 93 is less than 800.   ● True   ○ False

⑪ Find 4 × 7,342.

28200
1200
160
8
—————
29368

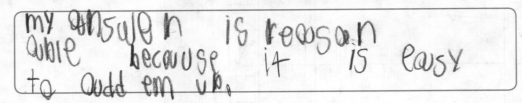

Use estimation to explain why your answer is reasonable.

my answen is reasonable because it is easy to add em up.

⑫ For Exercises 12a–12d, choose Yes or No to tell whether the equation is true.

12a. 5 × 60 = 30   ○ Yes   ● No

12b. 500 × 6 = 30,000   ○ Yes   ● No

12c. 50 × 60 = 3,000   ● Yes   ○ No

12d. 5 × 6,000 = 30,000   ● Yes   ○ No

⑬ The best estimate for 78 × 50 is that it must be greater than ___?___ but less than ___?___.

Select one number from each column to make the sentence true.

Greater than	Less than
○ 3,200	○ 3,200
● 3,500	○ 3,500
○ 4,000	● 4,000
○ 4,200	○ 4,200

⑭ Choose the number from the box to complete the statement.

The product of 39 and 22 is closest to [____].

300
(400)
800
8,000

15 A bus tour of New York City costs $48 per person. A group of 7 people go on the tour. What is the cost for the group? Explain how you found your answer.

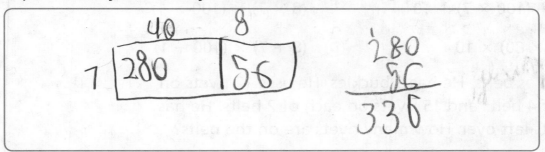

16 There is a book sale at the library. The price for each book is $4. If 239 books are sold, how much money will be made at the sale?

(A) $235

(B) $243

(C) $826

(D) $956

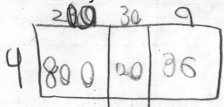

17 Volunteers are needed at the animal shelter. If 245 boys and 304 girls each volunteer to work 3 hours, how many volunteer hours is this?

Part A

Identify any extra information given in the problem. Explain your reasoning.

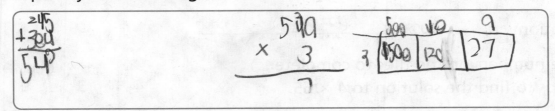

Part B

Solve the problem. Show your work.

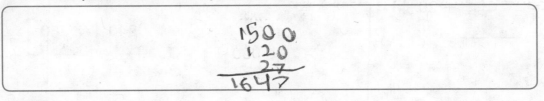

18 Select an expression that is equivalent to 7 × 800.
Mark all that apply.

Ⓐ 8 + (100 × 7) + 10   Ⓑ (8 × 7) × (100 × 1)

Ⓒ (7 × 80) × 10   Ⓓ (8 + 7) × (100 + 1)

19 ~~Joe makes belts.~~ He has 9 buckles. He uses 12 rivets on
each of 4 belts and 15 rivets on each of 2 belts. He has
22 rivets left over. How many rivets are on the belts?

Part A

Identify any extra information given in the problem.

Joe makes belts

Part B

Solve the problem. Show your work.

20 Draw an area model for 7 × 5,432. Then write an
equation to match your model.

Equation: _____7_____ × ___5,432___ = _____

21 Use the numbers on the tiles to complete
the steps to find the solution to 4 × 65.

4 × 65 = _____ × (60 + _____)

   = (4 × _____) + (4 × _____)

   = _____ + 20

   = _____

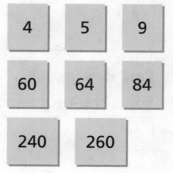

4	5	9
60	64	84
240	260	

Shop for a Clothing Drive

Mrs. Liston and 9 of her friends are
shopping for clothes to donate to a winter
clothing drive. The store has many clothing
items for sale. The table shows the items
Mrs. Liston and her friends can buy and the
price for each item.

Clothing for Sale

Item	Price
Shirt	$15
Jeans	$25
Sweater	$45
Boots	$75
Coat	$99

1 Mrs. Liston has $259. Is it possible for her to spend
the whole amount by buying only one kind of item
at the store? How do you know?

_____

_____

_____

_____

2 What are 2 different ways that Mrs. Liston can
spend $259 at the store?

_____

_____

3 If Mrs. Liston and her friends each spend $259 at the store,
how much money do they spend in all? How do you know?

_____

_____

4 Mrs. Liston collected $1,800 for the clothing drive. She buys
24 pairs of jeans and 24 sweaters. What could she buy with
the money that is left?

_____

_____

_____

_____

_____

The store puts some items on sale, as shown in the table.

Clothing for Sale

Item	Original Price	Sale Price
Shirt	$15	$12
Jeans	$25	
Sweater	$45	$42
Boots	$75	$56
Coat	$99	

5 How would these sale prices affect what Mrs. Liston could have bought with $1,800? Explain.

_____

_____

_____

_____

_____

6 Mrs. Liston and her friends would like to buy a shirt, a pair of jeans, and a sweater for 32 people. They will hold a dinner to raise the money needed to buy these items on sale. They plan to estimate the money needed. Will this help them set an appropriate goal for their dinner? Explain your decision.

_____

_____

_____

_____

7 Explain how to write a word problem that requires multiplication and addition to solve using the information in the table. Give a problem in your explanation.

_____

_____

_____

_____

_____

Dear Family:

Your child is familiar with multiplication from earlier units. Unit 3 of *Math Expressions* extends the concepts used in multiplication to teach your child division. The main goals of this unit are to:

• Learn methods for dividing whole numbers up to four digits.

• Use estimates to check the reasonableness of answers.

• Solve problems involving division and remainders.

Your child will learn and practice techniques such as the Place Value Sections, Expanded Notation, and Digit-by-Digit methods to gain speed and accuracy in division. At first, your child will learn to use patterns and multiplication to divide. Later, your child will learn to use the methods with divisors from 2 to 9. Then your child will learn to divide when there is a zero in the quotient or dividend and to watch out for potential problems involving these situations.

Examples of Division Methods:

Place Value Sections Method

$$
\begin{array}{c}
\quad 60 + \quad 6 = 66 \\
5\ \boxed{\begin{array}{c|c} 330 & 30 \\ -300 & -30 \\ \hline 30 & 0 \end{array}} \\
\end{array}
$$

Expanded Notation Method

$$
\begin{array}{r}
6\ \\
60\ \Big]\,66 \\
5\overline{)330} \\
-300 \\
\hline
30 \\
-30 \\
\hline
0
\end{array}
$$

Digit-by-Digit Method

$$
\begin{array}{r}
66 \\
5\overline{)330} \\
-30 \\
\hline
30 \\
-30 \\
\hline
0
\end{array}
$$

> Your child may use whatever method he or she chooses as long as he or she can explain it. Some children like to use different methods.

Your child will also learn to interpret remainders in the context of the problem being solved; for example, when the remainder alone is the answer to a word problem.

Finally, your child will apply this knowledge to solve mixed problems with one or more steps and using all four operations.

If you have questions or problems, please contact me.

Sincerely,
Your child's teacher

CC SS **Unit 3 addresses the following standards from the** Common Core State Standards for Mathematics: **4.OA.A.3, 4.NBT.A.3, 4.NBT.B.6 and all** Mathematical Practices.

Estimada familia:

En unidades anteriores su niño se ha familiarizado con la multiplicación. La Unidad 3 de *Math Expressions* amplía los conceptos usados en la multiplicación para que su niño aprenda la división. Los objetivos principales de esta unidad son:

• aprender métodos para dividir números enteros de hasta cuatro dígitos.

• usar la estimación para comprobar si las respuestas son razonables.

• resolver problemas que requieran división y residuos.

Su niño aprenderá y practicará técnicas tales como las de Secciones de valor posicional, Notación extendida y Dígito por dígito, para adquirir rapidez y precisión en la división. Al principio, su niño aprenderá a usar patrones y la multiplicación para dividir. Más adelante, usará los métodos con divisores de 2 a 9. Luego, aprenderá a dividir cuando haya un cero en el cociente o en el dividendo, y a detectar problemas que pueden surgir en esas situaciones.

Ejemplos de métodos de división:

Secciones de valor posicional	Notación extendida	Dígito por dígito

$$60 + 6 = 66$$

$$5 \overline{\begin{array}{c|c} 330 & 30 \\ -300 & 30 \\ \hline 30 & 0 \end{array}}$$

$$\begin{array}{r} 6 \\ 60 \end{array} \Big] 66$$

$$\begin{array}{r} 5\overline{)330} \\ -300 \\ \hline 30 \\ -30 \\ \hline 0 \end{array}$$

$$\begin{array}{r} 66 \\ 5\overline{)330} \\ -30 \\ \hline 30 \\ -30 \\ \hline 0 \end{array}$$

> Su niño puede usar el método que elija siempre y cuando pueda explicarlo. A algunos niños les gusta usar métodos diferentes.

Su niño también aprenderá a interpretar los residuos en el contexto del problema que se esté resolviendo; por ejemplo, cuando solamente el residuo es la respuesta a un problema.

Por último, su niño aplicará este conocimiento para resolver problemas mixtos de uno o más pasos, usando las cuatro operaciones.

Si tiene alguna pregunta o comentario, por favor comuníquese conmigo.

Atentamente,
El maestro de su niño

En la Unidad 3 se aplican los siguientes estándares de los Estándares estatales comunes de matemáticas: **4.OA.A.3, 4.NBT.A.3, 4.NBT.B.6 y todos los de** Prácticas matemáticas.

dividend

remainder

divisor

quotient

The number left over after dividing two numbers that are not evenly divisible.

Example:

8 R3

5$\overline{)43}$ The remainder is 3.

The number that is divided in division.

Example:

7

9$\overline{)63}$ 63 is the dividend.

The number you divide by in division.

Example:

7

9$\overline{)63}$ 9 is the divisor.

The answer to a division problem.

Example:

7

9$\overline{)63}$ 7 is the quotient.

© Houghton Mifflin Harcourt Publishing Company

Name _____

Division Vocabulary and Models

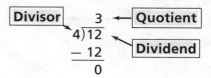

Although multiplication and division are inverse operations, each operation has its own language.

Multiplication Words

$$3 \leftarrow \text{Factor}$$
$$\times\ 4 \leftarrow \text{Factor}$$
$$\overline{12} \leftarrow \text{Product}$$

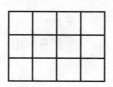

Factor $\rightarrow 3$
$4\overline{)12} \leftarrow$ Product
$-\ 12$
$\overline{\hphantom{-\ 1}0}$

Division Words

Divisor $\quad 3 \leftarrow$ Quotient
$4\overline{)12} \leftarrow$ Dividend
$-\ 12$
$\overline{\hphantom{-\ 1}0}$

The models for multiplication and division are the same models.

array

12 bottles on a table

$12 \div 3 =$ _____

$3 \times$ _____ $= 12$

rows and columns

12 tiles on a wall

$12 \div 3 =$ _____

$3 \times$ _____ $= 12$

area model
___ ft

3 ft | 12 sq ft

12 square feet of carpet

$12 \div 3 =$ _____

$3 \times$ _____ $= 12$

Discuss Remainders

Sometimes when you divide, some are left over. The left over amount is called the **remainder**.

If you have 14 juice boxes arranged in groups of 3, how many juice boxes will be left over?

$\begin{array}{r} 4\ R2 \\ 3\overline{)14} \\ -\ 12 \\ \hline 2 \end{array}$ ← 2 are left over.
2 is the remainder.

Compare the divisor and the remainder. The remainder must be less than the divisor.

2 < 3, so the remainder is correct.

**Multiply to check division.
Add the remainder.**

$4 \times 3 = 12$
$12 + 2 = 14$

Divide with Remainders

The remainder must be less than the divisor.
If it is not, increase the quotient.

$$
\begin{array}{r}
3 \\
5\overline{)23} \\
-15 \\
\hline
8 \text{ no} \\
8 > 5
\end{array}
\qquad\longrightarrow\qquad
\begin{array}{r}
4 \text{ R3} \\
5\overline{)23} \\
-20 \\
\hline
3 \text{ yes} \\
3 < 5
\end{array}
$$

$$
\begin{array}{r}
8 \\
9\overline{)87} \\
-72 \\
\hline
15 \text{ no} \\
15 > 9
\end{array}
\qquad\longrightarrow\qquad
\begin{array}{r}
9 \text{ R6} \\
9\overline{)87} \\
-81 \\
\hline
6 \text{ yes} \\
6 < 9
\end{array}
$$

Divide with remainders.

1 $2\overline{)19}$ **2** $7\overline{)50}$ **3** $9\overline{)48}$

Divide. Multiply to check the last problem in each row.

4 $6\overline{)27}$ $\begin{array}{r}4\text{R}3\\-24\\\hline 3\end{array}$

5 $4\overline{)30}$ $\begin{array}{r}7\text{R}2\\-28\\\hline 2\end{array}$

6 $7\overline{)39}$ $\begin{array}{r}5\text{ R4}\\-35\\\hline 4\end{array}$

$7 \cdot 5 + 4 =$
$35 + 4 = 39$

7 $8\overline{)43}$ $\begin{array}{r}5\text{R}3\\10\\\hline 3\end{array}$

8 $5\overline{)26}$ $\begin{array}{r}5\text{R}1\\-25\\\hline 1\end{array}$

9 $9\overline{)41}$

10 $5\overline{)32}$ **11** $4\overline{)21}$ **12** $3\overline{)22}$

Name _____

Multiply and Divide with Zeros

When you multiply or divide with zeros, you can see a pattern.

$4 \times 1 = 4$	$4 \div 4 = 1$	$7 \times 5 = 35$	$35 \div 7 = 5$
$4 \times 10 = 40$	$40 \div 4 = 10$	$7 \times 50 = 350$	$350 \div 7 = 50$
$4 \times 100 = 400$	$400 \div 4 = 100$	$7 \times 500 = 3,500$	$3,500 \div 7 = 500$
$4 \times 1,000 = 4,000$	$4,000 \div 4 = 1,000$	$7 \times 5,000 = 35,000$	$35,000 \div 7 = 5,000$

13 What pattern do you notice when you multiply with zeros?

_____

_____

14 What pattern do you notice when you divide with zeros?

_____

_____

Find the unknown factor. Multiply to check the division.

15 $4\overline{)320}$ $4 \cdot$ _____ $= 320$ **16** $6\overline{)420}$ $6 \cdot$ _____ $= 420$

17 $7\overline{)49}$ $7 \cdot$ _____ $= 49$ **18** $3\overline{)1,800}$ $3 \cdot$ _____ $= 1,800$

19 $5\overline{)4,500}$ $5 \cdot$ _____ $= 4,500$ **20** $9\overline{)3,600}$ $9 \cdot$ _____ $= 3,600$

21 $6\overline{)3,000}$ $6 \cdot$ _____ $= 3,000$ **22** $5\overline{)4,000}$ $5 \cdot$ _____ $= 4,000$

Divide with Zeros and Remainders

Divide. Multiply to check your answer.

23 $\begin{array}{r} 300 \text{ R6} \\ 7\overline{)2,106} \\ -2,100 \\ \hline 6 \end{array}$

24 $8\overline{)643}$

25 $9\overline{)275}$

26 $2\overline{)1,601}$

27 $3\overline{)1,802}$

28 $4\overline{)2,803}$

29 $5\overline{)4,503}$

30 $6\overline{)4,205}$

Check Understanding

Make a drawing to show $4\overline{)14}$. Your drawing should show an array and a remainder.

© Houghton Mifflin Harcourt Publishing Company

Name _____

Multiplying and Dividing

Complete the steps.

1 Sam divides 738 by 6. He uses the Place Value Sections Method and the Expanded Notation Method.

a. Sam thinks: I'll draw the Place Value Sections that I know from multiplication. To divide, I need to find how many hundreds, tens, and ones to find the unknown factor.

Place Value Sections Method   **Expanded Notation Method**

__ hundreds + __ tens + __ ones

	__00	__0	__
6	738		

$6\overline{)738}$

b. 6 × 100 = 600 will fit. 6 × 200 = 1,200 is too big.

	__00	+	__0	+	__
6	738				

$6\overline{)738}$

c. I have 138 left for the other sections.
6 × 20 = 120 will fit. 6 × 30 = 180 is too big.

	100	+	__0	+	__
6	738		138		
	−600				
	138				

$$\begin{array}{r} 100 \\ 6\overline{)738} \\ -600 \\ \hline 138 \end{array}$$

d. 6 × 3 = 18

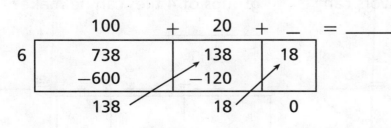

	100	+	20	+	__	=
6	738		138		18	
	−600		−120			
	138		18		0	

$$\begin{array}{r} \left.\begin{array}{r}20 \\ 100\end{array}\right] \\ 6\overline{)738} \\ -600 \\ \hline 138 \\ -120 \\ \hline 18 \end{array}$$

Practice the Place Value Sections Method

Solve. Use Place Value Sections Method for division.

The area of the new rectangular sidewalk at the mall will be 3,915 square feet. It will be 9 feet wide. How long will it be? __435 ft__

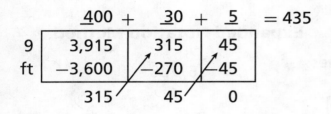

$$\underline{400} + \underline{30} + \underline{5} = 435$$

9 ft	3,915 −3,600	315 −270	45 −45
	315	45	0

2 The rectangular sidewalk at the theater will have an area of 2,748 square feet. It will be 6 feet wide. How long will it be? _____

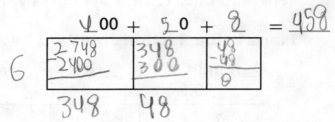

$$\underline{4}00 + \underline{5}0 + \underline{8} = 458$$

2,748 −2,400	348 −300	48 −48
348	48	0

3 Pens are packaged in boxes of 8. The store received a shipment of 4,576 pens. How many boxes of pens did they receive? _____

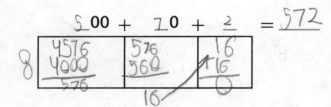

$$\underline{5}00 + \underline{7}0 + \underline{2} = 572$$

4576 4000	576 560	16 16
576	16	0

4 A factory has 2,160 erasers. They package them in groups of 5. How many packages of erasers does the factory have? _____

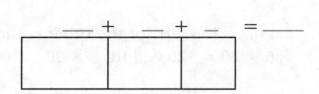

$$\underline{} + \underline{} + \underline{} = \underline{}$$

5 A party planner has 834 small flowers to make party favors. She will put 3 flowers in each party favor. How many party favors can she make? _____

$$\underline{} + \underline{} + \underline{} = \underline{}$$

6 An artist has 956 tiles to use in a design. He plans to arrange the tiles in groups of 4 tiles. How many groups of 4 tiles can he make? _____

$$\underline{} + \underline{} + \underline{} = \underline{}$$

Relate Three-Digit Multiplication to Division

Name _____

Problem Solving with Three-Digit Quotients

Solve using the Expanded Notation Method for division.

7 A toy company has 740 games to donate to different schools. Each school will receive 4 games. How many schools will receive games?

185

```
    5
  80 ] 185
 100
4)740
 -400
  340
 -320
   20
  -20
```

8 A landscape architect designs a rectangular garden that is 1,232 square feet. It is 8 feet wide. How long is the garden?

_____

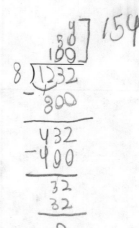

```
   4
  50 ] 154
 100
8)1232
  800
  432
 -400
   32
   32
    0
```

9 The convention center is expecting 1,434 people for an event. Since each table can seat 6 people, how many tables will the convention center need to set up?

_____

)

10 An adult lion weighs 375 pounds. A lion cub weighs 3 pounds. How many times the lion cub's weight is the adult lion's weight?

_____

)

Relate Three-Digit Multiplication to Division **123**

Practice with the Expanded Notation Method

Solve using the Expanded Notation Method for division.

⑪ 3)$\overline{552}$ ⑫ 7)$\overline{851}$ ⑬ 2)$\overline{978}$

⑭ 4)$\overline{979}$ ⑮ 3)$\overline{1,098}$ ⑯ 5)$\overline{2,945}$

⑰ 7)$\overline{1,652}$ ⑱ 6)$\overline{3,938}$

 Check Understanding
Explain how to relate multiplication to division using the Place Value Sections Method and the Expanded Notation Method.

Name _____

Two-Digit and Four-Digit Quotients

Solve. Use the Place Value Sections and the Expanded Notation Methods for division.

1   20 +   8 = 28

9	252	72
	− 180	− 72

72   0

9)252

2   _0_ +   __ = __

6	162	42
	-120	-42

42   0

6)162

-120

42

-42

0

3   __,000 +   __00 +   __0 +   __ = ____

8	8,984			

8)8,984

4   2,000 +   5_00 +   2_0 +   _4_ = 2879

3	7,722	1,722	222	12
	-6000	-1500	-210	-12

1722   222   12   0

508 ⌐
2000 ⌐ 2,57
3)7,722
  6000
 1722
-1500
 222
-210
  12
 -12
  0

Content Standards **4.NBT.B.6**
Mathematical Practices **MP2**, **MP3**, **MP6**, **MP7**, **MP8**

Finding Group Size

5 An orchard has 516 apples ready for delivery. There are the same number of apples in each of 4 crates. How many apples are in each crate?

$516 \div 4 = ?$

4 groups

$4\overline{)516}$

Divide 5 hundreds, 1 ten, 6 ones equally among 4 groups.

Complete the steps.

Step 1

4 groups

1 hundred
1 hundred
1 hundred
1 hundred

5 hundreds ÷ 4

Each group gets 1 hundred. 1 hundred is left.

$$\begin{array}{r} 1 \\ 4\overline{)516} \\ -4 \\ \hline 1 \end{array}$$

Regroup 1 hundred.

10 tens + 1 ten = 11 _____

$$\begin{array}{r} 1 \\ 4\overline{)516} \\ -4 \\ \hline 11 \end{array}$$

Step 2

4 groups

1 hundred + 2 tens
1 hundred + 2 tens
1 hundred + 2 tens
1 hundred + 2 tens

11 tens ÷ 4

Each group gets 2 tens. 3 _____ are left.

$$\begin{array}{r} 12 \\ 4\overline{)516} \\ -4 \\ \hline 11 \\ -8 \\ \hline 3 \end{array}$$

Regroup 3 tens.

30 ones + 6 ones = _____ ones

$$\begin{array}{r} 12 \\ 4\overline{)516} \\ -4 \\ \hline 11 \\ -8 \\ \hline 36 \end{array}$$

Step 3

4 groups

1 hundred + 2 tens + 9
1 hundred + 2 tens + 9
1 hundred + 2 tens + 9
1 hundred + 2 tens + 9

36 ones ÷ 4

Each group gets 9 ones. There are _____ ones left.

$$\begin{array}{r} 129 \\ 4\overline{)516} \\ -4 \\ \hline 11 \\ -8 \\ \hline 36 \\ -36 \\ \hline 0 \end{array}$$

There are _____ apples in each crate.

Discuss Two-Digit and Four-Digit Quotients

Name _____

Practice

Divide.

6 $4\overline{)868}$

7 $6\overline{)5,142}$

8 $3\overline{)4,395}$

9 $4\overline{)332}$

10 $7\overline{)1,617}$

11 $7\overline{)939}$

12 $2\overline{)4,276}$

13 $6\overline{)2,576}$

14 $7\overline{)441}$

15 $9\overline{)3,735}$

16 $7\overline{)406}$

17 $3\overline{)9,954}$

Discuss Two-Digit and Four-Digit Quotients **127**

Division Word Problems

Solve.

Show your work.

18 What is the length of a rectangle with an area of 756 square centimeters and a width of 4 centimeters?

?
4	756

_____

19 At a county fair, there are 7 booths that sell raffle tickets. In one day, 4,592 tickets were sold. Each booth sold the same number of tickets. How many tickets did each booth sell?

_____

20 One part of a city football stadium has 5,688 seats. The seats are arranged in 9 sections. Each section has the same number of seats. How many seats are in each section?

_____

21 An art museum has a total of 475 paintings hanging in 5 different viewing rooms. If each room has the same number of paintings, how many paintings are in each room?

_____

22 A parking garage can hold a total of 762 cars. The same number of cars can park on each floor. There are 6 floors. How many cars can park on each floor?

_____

 Check Understanding

For Problem 22, draw a model like the three-step model shown on page 126.

Discuss Two-Digit and Four-Digit Quotients

The Digit-by-Digit Method

1 Suppose Judith wants to divide 948 by 4. She knows how to use the Place Value Sections Method and the Expanded Notation Method, but she doesn't want to write all the zeros.

Place Value Sections Method

$$200 + \quad 30 + \quad 7 = 237$$

$$4 \begin{array}{|c|c|c|} \hline 948 & 148 & 28 \\ -800 & -120 & -28 \\ \hline \end{array}$$
$$\quad 148 \qquad 28 \qquad 0$$

Expanded Notation Method

$$\begin{array}{r} 7 \\ 30 \\ 200 \end{array} \Big] 237$$

$$\begin{array}{r} 4\overline{)948} \\ -800 \\ \hline 148 \\ -120 \\ \hline 28 \\ -28 \\ \hline 0 \end{array}$$

Judith thinks: I'll look at the place values in decreasing order. I'll imagine zeros in the other places, but I don't need to think about them until I'm ready to divide in that place.

Step 1: Look at the greatest place value first. Divide the hundreds. Then subtract.

9 hundreds ÷ 4 = 2 hundreds + 1 hundred left over

$$\begin{array}{r} 2 \\ 4\overline{)948} \\ -8 \\ \hline 1 \end{array}$$

Step 2: Bring down the 4. Divide the tens. Then subtract.

14 tens ÷ 4 = 3 tens + 2 tens left over

$$\begin{array}{r} 23 \\ 4\overline{)948} \\ -8\downarrow \\ \hline 14 \\ -12 \\ \hline 2 \end{array}$$

Step 3: Bring down the 8. Divide the ones. Then subtract.

28 ones ÷ 4 = 7 ones

$$\begin{array}{r} 237 \\ 4\overline{)948} \\ -8 \\ \hline 14 \\ -12\downarrow \\ \hline 28 \\ -28 \\ \hline 0 \end{array}$$

What's the Error?

Dear Math Students,

Here is a division problem I tried to solve.

$$
\begin{array}{r}
5{,}796 \\
3\overline{)1{,}738} \\
-15 \\
\hline
23 \\
-21 \\
\hline
28 \\
-27 \\
\hline
18 \\
-18 \\
\hline
0
\end{array}
$$

Is my answer correct? If not, please help
me understand why it is wrong.

Thank you,
Puzzled Penguin

2 **Write a response to Puzzled Penguin.**

_____

_____

_____

Solve. Use the Digit-by-Digit Method.

3 4$\overline{)3{,}036}$

4 7$\overline{)5{,}292}$

5 6$\overline{)853}$

Digit-by-Digit Method

Practice

Divide.

6 $5)\overline{965}$

7 $8)\overline{128}$

8 $8)\overline{928}$

9 $3)\overline{716}$

10 $4)\overline{4,596}$

11 $4)\overline{982}$

12 $3)\overline{6,342}$

13 $8)\overline{578}$

14 $5)\overline{1,155}$

15 $6)\overline{3,336}$

16 $7)\overline{672}$

17 $3)\overline{4,152}$

Solve Division Problems

Write an equation to represent the problem. Then, solve.

Show your work.

? cm

6 cm	528 sq cm

18 What is the length of a rectangle with an area of 528 square centimeters and a width of 6 centimeters?

_____

19 A cookbook features 414 recipes. There are 3 recipes on each page. How many pages are in the cookbook?

_____

20 A bus travels the same route once a day for 5 days. At the end of the fifth day, the bus has traveled 435 miles. How many miles does the bus travel each day?

_____

21 Ms. Tyler places a container of marbles at each table of 6 students. The students are told to share the marbles equally with the students at their table. If there are 714 marbles in the container, how many marbles should each student get?

_____

22 Sam's Used Bookstore is organizing their books on display shelves. They have 976 books and want 8 books displayed on each shelf. How many shelves will the books fill?

_____

✓ **Check Understanding**

Describe how to solve a division problem using the Digit-by-Digit Method.

Digit-by-Digit Method

Practice Division

Use any method to solve.

1. 8)960

2. 4)632

3. 7)809

4. 5)736

5. 4)3,068

6. 3)6,206

7. 2)6,476

8. 6)8,825

Solve Division Word Problems

9. A helper in the school store suggests selling notebooks in packages of 4. How many packages of 4 can be made from 192 notebooks?

10. Another helper suggests selling notebooks in packages of 6. How many packages of 6 can be made from 192 notebooks?

11. The store will sell packages of notebooks for $3.00 each.

   a. Which would be a better deal for students, packages of 4 or packages of 6?

   b. Which package size would make more money for the store?

Solve Division Word Problems (continued)

Another helper in the school store suggests making
packages of 7 or 8 notebooks.

Show your work.

12 How many packages of 7 notebooks can be made
from 896 notebooks? _____

13 How many packages of 8 notebooks can be made
from 896 notebooks? _____

14 The store will sell packages of notebooks for $6.00 each.

   a. Would you rather buy a package with 7 notebooks
or a package with 8 notebooks? Explain.

   _____

   _____

   b. Would packages of 7 notebooks or packages of
8 notebooks make more money for the store? Explain.

   _____

   _____

15 The students at Walnut Street School collected 2,790 cans
for a recycling center. Each student brought in 5 cans.
How many students attend the school?

_____

16 A cube can be made from 6 square cards that are
each the same size. How many cubes can be made
out of 7,254 cards?

_____

17 There are 5,896 beads in a barrel at a factory. These
beads will be sold in packets of 4. How many full packets
can be made from the beads in the barrel?

_____

✓**Check Understanding**

Solve the problem 6,584 ÷ 8 using any one of the methods
discussed in this lesson. Explain your steps. _____

Divide by Any Method

Check Quotients With Rounding and Estimation

Rounding and estimating can be used to check answers. Review your rounding skills, and then apply what you know to division problems.

Use rounding and estimating to decide whether each quotient makes sense.

1 $\overset{\text{18 R2}}{3)\overline{56}}$　　**2** $\overset{\text{92 R3}}{5)\overline{463}}$　　**3** $\overset{928}{6)\overline{5,568}}$　　**4** $\overset{\text{129 R4}}{7)\overline{907}}$

Practice Dividing and Estimating

Solve, using any method. Then check your answer by rounding and estimating.

5 $7)\overline{59}$

est: 8
8 R 3
-36
3
7×8=50

6 $3)\overline{72}$

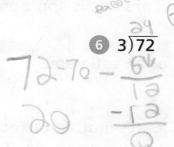

exact
24
est: 20
72-70
$6\downarrow$
$\overline{12}$
-12
0

7 $6)\overline{83}$

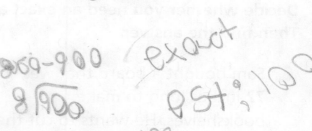

800-900
exact
est: 100
8)900

8 $7)\overline{628}$

9 $7)\overline{805}$

10 $8)\overline{869}$

108 R5
$-8\downarrow$
06
$-0\downarrow$
69
-64
5

11 $2)\overline{2,986}$

est: 800
6)5000

12 $6)\overline{4,652}$

775 R 2
42↓
45
$-42\downarrow$
32
-30
2

13 $7)\overline{7,310}$

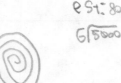

© Houghton Mifflin Harcourt Publishing Company

Estimate or Exact Answer

Some problems require an exact answer. Others require an estimate only.

Exact Answer If a problem asks for an exact answer, then you will have to do the calculation.

Example: The school cafeteria prepares 3,210 lunches each week. The same number of lunches are prepared 5 days each week. How many lunches are prepared each day?

Discuss why you think this problem requires an exact answer.

Estimate If a problem asks for a close answer and uses *about, approximately, almost,* or *nearly,* then you can estimate.

Example: Milo has to read a 229-page book. He has 8 days to finish it. About how many pages should he read each day?

Discuss why an estimate, and not an exact answer, is appropriate.

Decide whether you need an exact answer or an estimate. Then find the answer.

14 Sam bought a board that was 72 inches long to make bookshelves. He wants to cut the board into three equal pieces and use each one for a shelf. How long will each shelf be?

_____

15 Carl's mother baked 62 mini muffins for Carl's class. There are 18 people in his class, including the teacher. About how many mini muffins should each person get?

_____

16 Each 24-inch shelf can hold about 10 books. Approximately how many inches wide is each book?

_____

17 Malcom wants to buy 3 train tickets. Each ticket costs $45. How much money will he need?

_____

✓ **Check Understanding**

Describe one rounding method you used to estimate answers in this lesson.

Estimate to Check Quotients

Name _____

Different Kinds of Remainders

Remainders in division have different meanings, depending upon the type of problem you solve.

$$\begin{array}{r} 2 \text{ R1} \\ 4\overline{)9} \\ -8 \\ \hline 1 \end{array}$$

The same numeric solution shown at the right works for the following five problems. Describe why the remainder means something different in each problem.

A. **The remainder is not part of the question.** Thomas has one 9-foot pine board. He needs to make 4-foot shelves for his books. How many shelves can he cut? _____

_____

_____

B. **The remainder causes the answer to be rounded up.** Nine students are going on a field trip. Parents have offered to drive. If each parent can drive 4 students, how many parents need to drive? _____

_____

_____

C. **The remainder is a fractional part of the answer.** One Monday Kim brought 9 apples to school. She shared them equally among herself and 3 friends. How many apples did each person get? _____

_____

_____

_____

D. **The remainder is a decimal part of the answer.** Raul bought 4 toy cars for $9.00. Each car cost the same amount. How much did each car cost? _____

_____

_____

E. **The remainder is the only part needed to answer the question.** Nine students have signed up to run a relay race. If each relay team can have 4 runners, how many students cannot run in the race? _____

_____

_____

Discuss Real World Division Problems

Solve. Then discuss the meaning of the remainder.

1 Maddie tried to divide 160 stickers equally among herself and 5 friends. There were some stickers left over, so she kept them. How many stickers did Maddie get?

30 stickers

_1+5=6_   _26R4_
            _6)160_

2 Kendra bought a bag of 200 cheese crackers for her class. If each student gets 7 crackers, how many students are there? How many crackers are left over?

3 Jerry bought shelves to hold the 132 DVDs in his collection. Each shelf can fit 8 DVDs. How many full shelves will Jerry have?

17 Shervs

4 Racheed had 87 pennies. He divided them equally among his 4 sisters. How many pennies did Racheed have left after he gave his sisters their shares?

5 Mara wants to buy some new pencil boxes for her pencil collection. She has 47 pencils. If each pencil box holds 9 pencils, how many pencil boxes does Mara need to buy?

6 boxes

_5R2_
_9)47_

6 Henry's coin bank holds only nickels. Henry takes $4.42 to the bank to exchange for nickels only. How many nickels will he get from the bank?

Check Understanding

How do you know what to do with the remainder when you divide?

Make Sense of Remainders

Name _____

Mixed One-Step Word Problems

The fourth- and fifth-grade classes at Jackson Elementary School held a Just-for-Fun Winter Carnival. All of the students in the school were invited.

Decide what operation you need to use to solve each problem. Then solve the problem.

1 Two students from each fourth- and fifth-grade class were on the planning committee. If there were a total of 14 classes for the two grades, how many students planned the carnival?

$2 \times 14 = 28$

students

2 To advertise the carnival, students decorated 4 hallway bulletin boards. They started with 2,025 pieces of colored paper. When they finished, they had 9 pieces left. How many pieces of paper did they use?

_____

3 The parents ordered pizzas to serve at the carnival. Each pizza was cut into 8 slices. How many pizzas had to be ordered so that 1,319 people could each have one slice?

$1319 \div 8 = 164 R7$

165 pizzas

4 There were 822 students signed up to run in timed races. If exactly 6 students ran in each race, how many races were there?

_____

5 At the raffle booth, 364 fourth-graders each bought one ticket to win a new school supply set. Only 8 fifth-graders each bought a ticket. How many students bought raffle tickets altogether?

_____

6 Altogether, 1,263 students were enrolled in the first through fifth grades at Jackson School. On the day of the carnival, 9 students were absent. How many students could have participated in the carnival activities?

_____

Mixed Multistep Word Problems

Solve these problems about Pine Street School's Games Day.

7 At the start of the games, 193 fourth-graders signed up to play in three events. Eighty-seven played in the first event. The rest of the students were evenly divided between the second and third events. How many students played in the third event?

53 events

$193 - 87 = 106$ $106 \div 2 = 53$

8 Three teams stacked paper cups into pyramids. Each team had 176 cups to use. Team 1 used exactly half of their cups. Team 2 used four times as many cups as Team 3. Team 3 used 32 cups. Which team stacked the most cups?

_____

_____

9 A team from each school had 250 foam balls and a bucket. The Jackson team dunked 6 fewer balls than the Pine Street team. The Pine Street team dunked all but 8 of their balls. How many balls did the two teams dunk in all?

$250 - 8 = 242$ PS

$242 - 6 = 236$ J

_____

10 When the day was over, everybody had earned at least 1 medal, and 32 students each got 2 medals. In all, 194 each of gold, silver, and bronze medals were given out. How many students played in the games?

_____

_____

_____

✓ **Check Understanding**

In Problem 8, find which team stacked the most cups if each team had 260 cups to use.

_____

_____

Name _____

Division and Amusement Parks

There are many things to do at an amusement park: ride the rides, play some games, try new foods. Many people like to ride roller coasters while at the amusement park.

The top three tallest roller coasters in the world are in the United States. One of the tallest roller coasters is 456 feet tall and is located in Jackson, New Jersey.

The fourth and fifth grade classes went on a field trip to the amusement park.

Show your work.

1. There are 58 fourth-grade students who are in line to ride the Loop-the-Loop roller coaster. Each roller coaster car holds 4 people. How many roller coaster cars are needed so they all can ride the roller coaster at the same time?

_____

2. Forty-one people are riding the Mile Long wooden roller coaster. Each roller coaster car holds 6 people. All the cars are full except the last car. How many people are in the last car?

_____

More Amusement Park Fun

After riding the roller coasters, the fourth and fifth grade classes spend the rest of the day getting lunch, going shopping, and riding the rest of the rides at the amusement park.

Solve.

Show your work.

3 There are 27 students in Evan's group. Each student decides to get a lunch special at the food stand. If each lunch special is $7, how much did the students spend for lunch altogether?

_____

4 Thirty-one students are in line to ride the Ferris wheel. Four students are needed to fill each Ferris wheel car. How many Ferris wheel cars will be full?

_____

5 In the souvenir shop, a worker opens a box of posters. The posters in the box are bundled in groups of 8. There are a total of 2,864 posters in a box. How many bundles of posters are in the box?

_____

Focus on Mathematical Practices

Make a Reading Plan

Matthew has 63 pages to read in 2–5 days. He wants to read the same number of pages each day and the greatest number of pages in the fewest days possible.

1 What is the best number of days for Matthew's reading plan?

_____

_____

2 How did you decide?

_____

_____

_____

_____

Sophia has 131 pages to read in 2–5 days.

3 Would it be possible for her to read the same number of pages each day? Explain.

_____

_____

4 Sophia decides to read the same number of pages on as many days as possible. What reading plan could Sophia follow? Show work to support your answer.

_____

_____

_____

_____

5 Suppose Sophia read 23 pages on the first day. She plans to read the remaining pages in 3–5 days. She wants to read the same number of pages on each of these days and the greatest number of pages in the fewest days possible. What is the best choice for the number of days for Sophia's reading plan? Explain how you decided.

_____

_____

_____

_____

_____

_____

_____

6 Explain how to write your own division problem with any given quotient and remainder. Give an example that includes the relationship between multiplication and division in your explanation.

_____

_____

_____

_____

_____

_____

_____

Dear Family:

In Unit 4 of *Math Expressions,* your child will apply the skills he or she has learned about operations with whole numbers while solving real world problems involving addition, subtraction, multiplication, and division.

Your child will simplify and evaluate expressions. Parentheses will be introduced to show which operation should be done first. The symbols "=" and "≠" will be used to show whether numbers and expressions are equal.

Other topics of study in this unit include situation and solution equations for addition and subtraction, as well as multiplication and division. Your child will use situation equations to represent real world problems and solution equations to solve the problems. This method of representing a problem is particularly helpful when the problems contain greater numbers and students cannot solve mentally.

Your child will also solve multiplication and addition comparison problems and compare these types of problems, identifying what is the same or different.

Addition Comparison	Multiplication Comparison
Angela is 14 years old. She is 4 years older than Damarcus. How old is Damarcus?	Shawn colored 5 pages in a coloring book. Anja colored 4 times as many pages as Shawn colored. How many pages did Anja color?

Students learn that in the addition problem they are adding 4, while in the multiplication problem, they are multiplying by 4.

Your child will apply this knowledge to solve word problems using all four operations and involving one or more steps.

Finally, your child will find factor pairs for whole numbers and generate and analyze numerical and geometric patterns.

If you have any questions or comments, please contact me.

Sincerely,
Your child's teacher

CC SS **Unit 4 addresses the following standards from the** Common Core State Standards for Mathematics: **4.OA.A.1, 4.OA.A.2, 4.OA.A.3, 4.OA.B.4, 4.OA.C.5, 4.NBT.B.4, 4.NBT.B.5, 4.NBT.B.6, 4.MD.A.2 and all** Mathematical Practices.

Estimada familia:

En la Unidad 4 de Math Expressions, su hijo aplicará las destrezas relacionadas con operaciones de números enteros que ha adquirido, resolviendo problemas cotidianos que involucran suma, resta, multiplicación y división.

Su hijo simplificará y evaluará expresiones. Se introducirán los paréntesis como una forma de mostrar cuál operación deberá completarse primero. Los signos "=" y "≠" se usarán para mostrar si los números o las expresiones son iguales o no.

Otros temas de estudio en esta unidad incluyen ecuaciones de situación y de solución para la suma y resta, así como para la multiplicación y división. Su hijo usará ecuaciones de situación para representar problemas de la vida cotidiana y ecuaciones de solución para resolver esos problemas. Este método para representar problemas es particularmente útil cuando los problemas involucran números grandes y los estudiantes no pueden resolverlos mentalmente.

Su hijo también resolverá problemas de comparación de multiplicación y suma, y comparará este tipo de problemas para identificar las semejanzas y diferencias.

Comparación de suma	Comparación de multiplicación
Ángela tiene 14 años. Ella es 4 años mayor que Damarcus. ¿Cuántos años tiene Damarcus?	Shawn coloreó 5 páginas de un libro. Ana coloreó 4 veces ese número de páginas. ¿Cuántas páginas coloreó Ana?

Los estudiantes aprenderán que en el problema de suma están sumando 4, mientras que en el problema de multiplicación, están multiplicando por 4.

Su hijo aplicará estos conocimientos para resolver problemas de uno o más pasos usando las cuatro operaciones.

Finalmente, su hijo hallará pares de factores para números enteros y generará y analizará patrones numéricos y geométricos.

Si tiene alguna pregunta por favor comuníquese conmigo.

Atentamente,
El maestro de su niño

© Houghton Mifflin Harcourt Publishing Company

En la Unidad 4 se aplican los siguientes estándares de los Estándares estatales comunes de matemáticas: **4.OA.A.1, 4.OA.A.2, 4.OA.A.3, 4.OA.B.4, 4.OA.C.5, 4.NBT.B.4, 4.NBT.B.5, 4.NBT.B.6, 4.MD.A.2 y todos los de** Prácticas matemáticas.

160 UNIT 4 LESSON 1 · Properties and Algebraic Notation

compare

equation

composite number

evaluate an expression

difference

expression

A statement that two expressions are equal. It has an equal sign.

Example:

$32 + 35 = 67$

$67 = 32 + 34 + 1$

$(7 \times 8) + 1 = 57$

Describe quantities as greater than, less than, or equal to each other.

Substitute a value for a letter (or symbol) and then simplify the expression.

A number greater than 1 that has more than one factor pair. Examples of composite numbers are 10 and 18. The factor pairs of 10 are 1 and 10, 2 and 5. The factor pairs of 18 are 1 and 18, 2 and 9, 3 and 6.

A number, variable, or a combination of numbers and variables with one or more operations.

Example:

4

$6x$

$6x - 5$

$7 + 4$

The result of a subtraction.

Example:

$54 - 37 = 17$ ◄——— difference

factor pair	pictograph
multiple	prime number
pattern	simplify an expression

A graph that uses pictures or symbols to represent data.

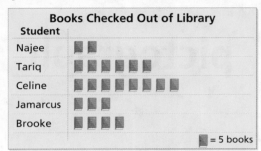

A factor pair for a number is a pair of whole numbers whose product is that number.

Example:

$$5 \times 7 = 35$$

factor product
pair

A number greater than 1 that has 1 and itself as the only factor pair. Examples of prime numbers are 2, 7, and 13. The only factor pair of 7 is 1 and 7.

A number that is the product of a given number and any whole number.

Examples:
$4 \times 1 = 4$, so 4 is a multiple of 4.
$4 \times 2 = 8$, so 8 is a multiple of 4.

Combining like terms and performing operations until all possible terms have been combined.

A sequence that can be described by a rule.

sum

term

The answer when adding
two or more addends.

Example:

$$53 + 26 = 79$$

addend   addend   sum

A number, variable, product,
or quotient in an expression
or equation. Each term is
separated by an operation
sign $(+, -)$.

Example:

$3n + 5$ has two terms, $3n$ and 5.

Name _____

Properties and Algebraic Notation

An **expression** is one or more numbers, variables, or numbers and variables with one or more operations.

Examples: 4   6x   6x − 5   7 + 4

An **equation** is a statement that two expressions are equal. It has an equal sign.

Examples: $40 + 25 = 65$
$(16 \div 4) - 3 = 1$

We **simplify an expression** or equation by performing operations to combine like **terms**.

Use the Identity Property to simplify each expression.

① $n + 5n$ _____ ② $17t + t$ _____ ③ $x + 245x$ _____

④ $9e - e$ _____ ⑤ $8c + c + c$ _____ ⑥ $(5z - z) - z$ _____

Solve.

⑦ $30 \div (35 \div 7) =$ _____ ⑧ $(72 \div 9) \div 4 =$ _____

⑨ $80 \div (32 \div 8) =$ _____ ⑩ $13 - (9 - 1) =$ _____

⑪ $(600 - 400) - 10 =$ _____ ⑫ $100 - (26 - 6) =$ _____

Use properties to find the value of ▪ or a.

⑬ $49 + 17 = ▪ + 49$ ⑭ $(a \cdot 2) \cdot 3 = 4 \cdot (2 \cdot 3)$ ⑮ $▪ \cdot 6 = 6 \cdot 8$

$▪ =$ _____ $a =$ _____ $▪ =$ _____

⑯ $6 \cdot (40 + a) = (6 \cdot 40) + (6 \cdot 5)$ ⑰ $(▪ \cdot 5) + (▪ \cdot 9) = 7 \cdot (5 + 9)$

$a =$ _____ $▪ =$ _____

⑱ $29 + 8 = ▪ + 29$ ⟶ Is $▪ = 4 + 2$ or $4 \cdot 2$? _____

⑲ $a \cdot 14 = 14 \cdot 15$ ⟶ Is $a = 5 \cdot 3$ or $5 + 3$? _____

⑳ $60 + 10 = ▪ + 60$ ⟶ Is $▪ = 2 + 5$ or $2 \cdot 5$? _____

© Houghton Mifflin Harcourt Publishing Company

Parentheses in Equations

Solve.

(21) $9 \cdot n = 144$

$n =$ _____

(22) $s + 170 = 200$

$s =$ _____

(23) $105 \div h = 7$

$h =$ _____

(24) $9 \cdot (6 + 2) = \blacksquare \cdot 8$

$\blacksquare =$ _____

(25) $\blacksquare \cdot 6 = 96$

$\blacksquare =$ _____

(26) $(15 \div 3) \cdot (4 + 1) = v$

$v =$ _____

(27) $(12 - 5) - (12 \div 6) =$ _____

(28) $(23 + 4) \div (8 - 5) =$ _____

(29) $(24 \div 3) \cdot (12 - 7) =$ _____

(30) $(22 + 8) \div (17 - 11) =$ _____

Substitute a Value

To **evaluate an expression** or equation, substitute a value for a letter (or symbol) and then simplify the expression by performing the operations.

Evaluate each expression.

(31) $a = 4$

$19 - (a + 6)$

_____

(32) $a = 10$

$(80 \div a) - 5$

_____

(33) $b = 3$

$(8 \div 4) \cdot (7 - b)$

_____

(34) $b = 7$

$21 \div (b - 4)$

_____

(35) $b = 11$

$(b + 9) \div (7 - 2)$

_____

(36) $c = 8$

$(20 - 10) + (7 + c)$

_____

(37) $x = 9$

$16 \cdot (13 - x)$

_____

(38) $d = 3$

$(24 \div 3) \cdot (d + 7)$

_____

(39) $d = 0$

$(63 \div 7) \cdot d$

_____

✓**Check Understanding**

Explain the steps you used to evaluate Exercise 32.

Properties and Algebraic Notation

Name _____

Discuss the = and ≠ Signs

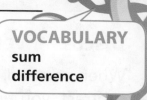

VOCABULARY
sum
difference

An equation is made up of two equal quantities or expressions. An equal sign (=) is used to show that the two sides of the equation are equal.

$$5 = 3 + 2 \qquad 3 + 2 = 5 \qquad 5 = 5 \qquad 3 + 2 = 2 + 3 \qquad 7 - 2 = 1 + 1 + 3$$

The "is not equal to" sign (≠) shows that two quantities are not equal.

$$4 \neq 3 + 2 \qquad 5 \neq 3 - 1 \qquad 5 \neq 4 \qquad 3 - 2 \neq 1 + 3 \qquad 3 + 2 \neq 1 + 1 + 2$$

An equation can have one or more numbers or letters on each side of the equal sign. A **sum** or **difference** can be written on either side of the equal sign.

1 Use the = sign to write four equations. Vary how many numbers you have on each side of your equations.

_____   _____

_____   _____

2 Use the ≠ sign to write four "is not equal to" statements. Vary how many numbers you have on each side of your statements.

_____   _____

_____   _____

Write = or ≠ to make each statement true.

3 $5 + 2 + 6$ ____ $6 + 7$

4 80 ____ $60 - 20$

5 70 ____ $40 + 30$

6 $18 - 4 + 11$ ____ 3

7 50 ____ $55 - (10 + 5)$

8 $21 + 6$ ____ $31 - 4$

Discuss Inverse Operations

When you add, you put two groups together. When you subtract, you find an unknown addend or take away one group from another. Addition and subtraction are inverse operations. They undo each other.

Addends are numbers that are added to make a sum. You can find two addends for a sum by breaking apart the number.

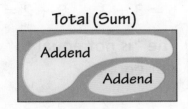

A break-apart drawing can help you find all eight related addition and subtraction equations for two addends.

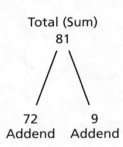

$$81 = 72 + 9 \qquad 72 + 9 = 81$$

$$81 = 9 + 72 \qquad 9 + 72 = 81$$

$$72 = 81 - 9 \qquad 81 - 9 = 72$$

$$9 = 81 - 72 \qquad 81 - 72 = 9$$

9 Which equations show the Commutative Property?

_____

_____

10 What is the total in each equation? Where is the total in a subtraction equation?

_____

_____

Solve each equation.

11 $50 = 30 + p$

$p =$ _____

12 $q + 20 = 60$

$q =$ _____

13 $90 - v = 50$

$v =$ _____

14 Write the eight related addition and subtraction equations for the break-apart drawing.

_____   _____

_____   _____

_____   _____

_____   _____

Situation and Solution Equations for Addition and Subtraction

Write Equations to Solve Problems

A situation equation shows the structure of the information in a problem. A solution equation shows the operation that can be used to solve a problem.

Write an equation to solve the problem. Draw a model if you need to.

Show your work.

15 In a collection of 2,152 coins, 628 coins are pennies. How many coins are not pennies?

_____

_____

16 Susanna took $3,050 out of her bank account. Now she has $11,605 left in the account. How much money was in Susanna's account to start?

_____

_____

17 In the month of May, Movieland rented 563 action movies and 452 comedy movies. How many action and comedy movies in all did Movieland rent in May?

_____

_____

Practice Solving Problems

Write an equation to solve the problem. Draw a model if you need to.

18 The workers at a factory made 3,250 pink balloons in the morning. There were 5,975 pink balloons at the factory at the end of the day. How many pink balloons did the factory workers make in the afternoon?

_____

_____

Practice Solving Problems (continued)

Show your work.

19 Terrence is planning a 760-mile trip. He travels 323 miles the first two days. How many miles does Terrence have left to travel on this trip?

_____

20 There were some people at the football stadium early last Sunday, and then 5,427 more people arrived. Then there were 79,852 people at the stadium. How many people arrived early?

_____

What's the Error?

Dear Math Students,

The problem below was part of my homework assignment.

Mrs. Nason had a collection of 1,845 stamps. She bought some more stamps. Now she has 2,270 stamps. How many stamps did Mrs. Nason buy?

To solve the problem, I wrote this equation:
$s - 1,845 = 2,270$. I solved the equation and wrote $s = 4,115$.

My teacher says that my answer is not correct. Can you help me understand what I did wrong and explain how to find the correct answer?

Your friend,
Puzzled Penguin

21 Write a response to Puzzled Penguin.

_____

_____

_____

 Check Understanding

Explain the difference between a situation equation and a solution equation. Use Puzzled Penguin's homework problem to give examples of each type of equation.

Situation and Solution Equations for Addition and Subtraction

Discuss Inverse Operations

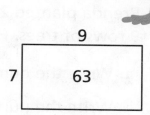

VOCABULARY
factor pair

Multiplication and division are inverse operations.
They undo each other.

A **factor pair** for a number is a pair of whole
numbers whose product is that number. For
example, a factor pair for 15 is 3 and 5. A rectangle
model is a diagram that shows a factor pair and the
product.

	9
7	63

1 Which numbers in the rectangle model above are
the factors? Where are the factors located?

_____

2 Which number is the product? Where is the product
located?

_____

A rectangle model can you help you find all eight related
multiplication and division equations for two factors. You
can write these equations for the rectangle model above.

$$63 = 7 \times 9 \qquad\qquad 7 \times 9 = 63$$
$$63 = 9 \times 7 \qquad\qquad 9 \times 7 = 63$$
$$7 = 63 \div 9 \qquad\qquad 63 \div 9 = 7$$
$$9 = 63 \div 7 \qquad\qquad 63 \div 7 = 9$$

3 Write the eight related multiplication and division
equations for the rectangle model below.

	12
8	96

_____   _____

_____   _____

_____   _____

_____   _____

Write Equations to Solve Problems

Read the problem. Complete the steps to solve.

n

9	234

4 Brenda planted 234 trees on her farm. The farm has 9 rows of trees. How many trees are in each row?

  a. Write the number of trees on the farm. _____

  b. Write the number of rows of trees. _____

  c. The number of trees in each row is unknown. Use the letter n to represent the number of trees in each row. Write a situation equation to solve the problem. _____

  d. Write a solution equation. _____

  e. Solve your equation. _____

Write an equation to solve the problem. Draw a model if you need to.

Show your work.

5 Evan is starting a cycling program. He will ride 315 miles each month for the next 6 months. How many miles does he plan to ride in all?

_____

6 Suki has 152 stickers to place in a sticker album. How many pages will Suki fill with stickers if she puts 8 stickers on each page?

_____

7 Al designed a wall pattern with 27 rows of 28 squares. How many squares are in the wall pattern?

_____

✓ Check Understanding

In Problem 6, if Suki had 248 stickers, how many pages in her album would be filled? _____

Situation and Solution Equations for Multiplication and Division

Solve for ▨ **or** *n*.

1. $84 \div n = 6$

   $n =$ _____

2. $(14 + 7) \cdot 8 = $ ▨ $\cdot 8$

   ▨ $=$ _____

Write an equation to show the problem. Then solve.   *Show your work.*

3. Miguel drove 197 miles on Monday. He drove some more miles on Tuesday. He drove 542 miles in all. How many miles did Miguel drive on Tuesday?

   _____

   _____

4. A theater has a seating capacity of 748 seats. If 3 performances are sold out, how many tickets are sold?

   _____

   _____

5. Britney is saving $996 to pay for summer camp. She wants to save the same amount of money each month for 6 months. How much money does Britney need to save each month?

   _____

   _____

Name _____ **Date** _____

Add or subtract.

1
```
  242
+ 316
```

2
```
  681
- 375
```

3
```
  2,945
+   713
```

4
```
  5,839
- 3,427
```

5
```
  17,649
+  2,431
```

6
```
  48,600
- 29,728
```

7
```
  6,739
+ 3,847
```

8
```
  5,069
- 4,853
```

9
```
  371
+ 542
```

10
```
  574
- 350
```

11
```
  26,366
-  7,382
```

12
```
  34,278
+ 57,341
```

13
```
  693,317
-  47,592
```

14
```
  242,730
+  79,527
```

15
```
  809,411
- 472,389
```

Name _____

Discuss Comparison Problems

VOCABULARY
compare

To prepare for a family gathering, Sara and Ryan made soup. Sara made 2 quarts. Ryan made 6 quarts.

You can **compare** amounts, using multiplication and division.

Let r equal the number of quarts Ryan made.
Let s equal the number of quarts Sara made.

Ryan made 3 times as many quarts as Sara.

$$r = 3 \cdot s, \; r = 3s, \text{ or } s = r \div 3$$

Ryan (r) | 2 | 2 | 2 | 6

Sarah (s) | 2

Solve.

Natasha made 12 quarts of soup. Manuel made 3 quarts.

1. Draw comparison bars to show the amount of soup each person made.

2. _____ made 4 times as many quarts as _____.

3. Write a multiplication equation that compares the amounts.

_____

4. Write a division equation that compares the amounts.

_____

5. Multiplication is the putting together of equal groups. How can this idea be used to explain why a *times as many* comparing situation is multiplication?

_____

_____

Share Solutions

Write an equation to solve each problem.
Draw a model if you need to.

Show your work.

6 There are 24 students in the science club. There are 2 times as many students in the drama club. How many students are in the drama club?

   a. Draw comparison bars to compare the numbers of students in each club.

   b. Write an equation to solve the problem.

   _____

7 There are 180 pennies in Miguel's coin collection and that is 5 times as many as the number of quarters in his coin collection. How many quarters does Miguel have?

   _____

8 Fred has 72 football cards and Scott has 6 football cards. The number of cards Fred has is how many times the number Scott has?

   _____

9 Audrey has 1,263 centimeters of fabric, and that is 3 times as much fabric as she needs to make some curtains. How many centimeters of fabric does Audrey need to make the curtains?

   _____

Check Understanding

Draw comparison bars to represent Problem 8 and the solution.

Multiplication Comparisons

Name _____

Discuss Comparison Situations

In Lesson 4-4, you learned about multiplication and division comparison situations. You can also compare by using addition and subtraction. You can find *how much more* or *how much less* one amount is than another.

The amount more or less is called the difference. In some problems, the difference is not given. You have to find it. In other problems, the lesser or the greater amount is not given.

Mai has 9 apples and 12 plums.

- How many more plums than apples does Mai have?

- How many fewer apples than plums does Mai have?

Plums	12

| Apples | 9 | *d* |

Comparison bars can help us show which amount is more. We show the difference in an oval.

Draw comparison bars for each problem. Write and solve an equation. Discuss other equations you could use.

1 A nursery has 70 rose bushes and 50 tea-tree bushes. How many fewer tea-tree bushes than rose bushes are at the nursery?

2 Dan wants to plant 30 trees. He has dug 21 holes. How many more holes does Dan need to dig?

Share Solutions

Draw comparison bars for each problem.
Write and solve an equation.

Show your models here.

3 Kyle and Maya are playing a computer game. Kyle scored 7,628 points. Maya scored 2,085 fewer points than Kyle. How many points did Maya score?

_____

_____

4 The school fair fundraiser made $632 more from baked goods than from games. The school fair made $935 from games. How much money did the school fair make from baked goods?

_____

_____

5 A college football stadium in Michigan seats 109,901 people. A college football stadium in Louisiana seats 92,542 people. How many fewer people does the stadium in Louisiana seat than the stadium in Michigan?

_____

_____

6 The soccer team drilled for 150 minutes last week. The team drilled for 30 minutes more than it scrimmaged. For how long did the team scrimmage?

_____

_____

Discuss Comparison Problems

Name _____

Solve Comparison Problems

For each problem, draw a model and write *addition* **or** *multiplication* **to identify the type of comparison. Then write and solve an equation to solve the problem.**

Show your models here.

7 Nick and Liz both collect marbles. Liz has 4 times as many marbles as Nick. If Nick has 240 marbles, how many marbles does Liz have?

Type of comparison: _____

Equation and answer: _____

8 Samantha has 145 fewer songs on her portable media player than Luke has on his portable media player. If Samantha has 583 songs, how many songs does Luke have?

Type of comparison: _____

Equation and answer: _____

9 A large bookstore sold 19,813 books on Saturday and 22,964 books on Sunday. How many fewer books did the bookstore sell on Saturday than on Sunday?

Type of comparison: _____

Equation and answer: _____

_____

10 Last weekend, Mr. Morgan rode his bike 3 miles. This weekend, he rode his bike 21 miles. How many times as many miles did Mr. Morgan ride his bike this weekend as last weekend?

Type of comparison: _____

Equation and answer: _____

_____

Practice

Write and solve an equation to solve each problem.
Draw comparison bars when needed.

Show your work.

11 On the last day of school, 100 more students wore
shorts than wore jeans. If 130 students wore jeans,
how many students wore shorts?

_____

12 Matthew completed a puzzle with 90 pieces. Wendy
completed a puzzle with 5 times as many pieces.
How many pieces are in Wendy's puzzle?

_____

13 There were 19,748 adults at a baseball game. There
were 5,136 fewer children at the baseball game than
adults. How many children were at the baseball game?

_____

What's the Error?

Dear Math Students,

I was asked to find the number of stamps that
Amanda has if her friend Jesse has 81 stamps and
that is 9 times as many stamps as Amanda has.

I wrote 81 × 9 = s. So, s = 729. My teacher says that my
answer is not correct. Can you explain what I did wrong?

Your friend,
Puzzled Penguin

14 Write a response to Puzzled Penguin.

_____

_____

 Check Understanding
Explain how addition comparison problems differ from
multiplication comparison problems.

Discuss Comparison Problems

Name _____

Use a Pictograph

A **pictograph** is a graph that uses pictures or symbols to represent data. This pictograph shows how many books 5 students checked out of a library in one year.

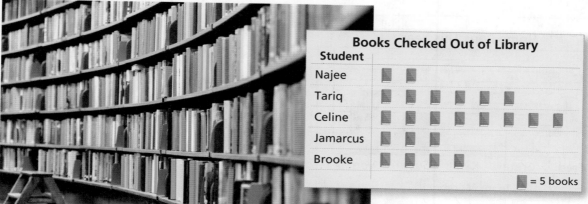

Books Checked Out of Library

Student							
Najee	▪	▪					
Tariq	▪	▪	▪	▪	▪	▪	
Celine	▪	▪	▪	▪	▪	▪	▪
Jamarcus	▪	▪	▪				
Brooke	▪	▪	▪	▪			

▪ = 5 books

Use the pictograph to solve.

1 Write an addition equation and a subtraction equation that compare the number of books Tariq checked out (*t*) with the number of books Jamarcus checked out (*j*).

_____

2 Write a multiplication equation and a division equation that compare the number of books Najee checked out (*n*) with the number of books Celine checked out (*c*).

_____

3 Celine checked out twice as many books as which student?

_____

4 Which student checked out 30 fewer books than Celine?

_____

5 The number of books Dawson checked out is not shown. If Jamarcus checked out 10 more books than Dawson, how many books did Dawson check out?

_____

Use a Bar Graph

The bar graph below shows the number of home runs hit by five members of a baseball team.

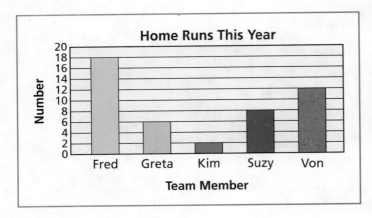

Use the bar graph to solve.

6 Write an addition equation and a subtraction equation that compare the number of home runs Suzy hit (*s*) with the number of home runs Kim hit (*k*).

_____

7 Write a multiplication equation and a division equation that compare the number of home runs Greta hit (*g*) with the number of runs Fred hit (*f*).

_____

8 How many more home runs did Von hit than Greta? _____

9 Which player hit 10 fewer home runs than Von? _____

10 This year, Fred hit 2 times as many home runs as he hit last year. How many home runs did Fred hit last year? _____

✓ Check Understanding

Use the bar graph to solve. This year, Kim hit 8 fewer home runs than she hit last year. How many home runs did Kim hit last year?

_____

Graphs and Comparison Problems

Name _____

Date _____

Write an equation.

1 Nicole swims 6 times as many laps as Evan. What multiplication equation compares the laps Nicole and Evan swim?

_____

Write an equation to show the problem. Then solve.

Show your work.

2 There are 34 hats at a shop. There are 2 times as many scarves as hats at the shop. How many scarves are at the shop?

_____

3 Liam has 51 stickers. He has 3 times as many stickers as Jade. How many stickers does Jade have?

_____

4 There are 16,492 people at a car race. There are 3,271 fewer people at the race this year than last year. How many people were at the car race last year?

_____

Use the bar graph. Write an equation to solve the problem.

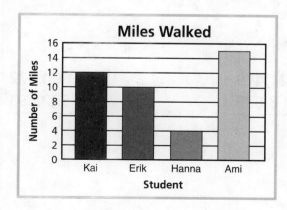

5 Kai walked how many times as many miles as Hanna?

_____

Name

Date

Add or subtract.

1
$$\begin{array}{r} 214 \\ + 180 \\ \hline \end{array}$$

2
$$\begin{array}{r} 427 \\ - 345 \\ \hline \end{array}$$

3
$$\begin{array}{r} 4{,}592 \\ + 3{,}667 \\ \hline \end{array}$$

4
$$\begin{array}{r} 6{,}953 \\ - 3{,}812 \\ \hline \end{array}$$

5
$$\begin{array}{r} 8{,}931 \\ + 658 \\ \hline \end{array}$$

6
$$\begin{array}{r} 50{,}730 \\ - 42{,}694 \\ \hline \end{array}$$

7
$$\begin{array}{r} 83{,}314 \\ + 20{,}894 \\ \hline \end{array}$$

8
$$\begin{array}{r} 9{,}063 \\ - 1{,}842 \\ \hline \end{array}$$

9
$$\begin{array}{r} 397 \\ + 411 \\ \hline \end{array}$$

10
$$\begin{array}{r} 694 \\ - 642 \\ \hline \end{array}$$

11
$$\begin{array}{r} 76{,}836 \\ - 8{,}565 \\ \hline \end{array}$$

12
$$\begin{array}{r} 367{,}530 \\ + 246{,}597 \\ \hline \end{array}$$

13
$$\begin{array}{r} 477{,}713 \\ - 80{,}722 \\ \hline \end{array}$$

14
$$\begin{array}{r} 21{,}419 \\ + 8{,}639 \\ \hline \end{array}$$

15
$$\begin{array}{r} 804{,}672 \\ - 522{,}891 \\ \hline \end{array}$$

Discuss the Steps of the Problem

Sometimes you will need to work through more than one step to solve a problem. The steps can be shown in one or more equations.

Solve.

1 At Parkes Elementary School, there are 6 fourth-grade classes with 17 students in each class. On Friday, 23 fourth graders brought lunch from home and the rest of the students bought lunch in the cafeteria. How many fourth graders bought lunch in the cafeteria on Friday?

_____

2 Solve the problem again by finishing Tommy's and Lucy's methods. Then discuss how the two methods are alike and how they are different.

Tommy's Method	Lucy's Method
Write an equation for each step.	**Write an equation for the whole problem.**
Find the total number of students who are in fourth grade.	Let n = the number of students who bought lunch.
$6 \times 17 =$ _____	Students in each fourth-grade class Students who brought lunch from home
Subtract the number of students who brought lunch from home.	$6 \quad \times$ _____ $-$ _____ $= n$
$102 - 23 =$ _____	_____ $= n$

3 Use an equation to solve. Discuss the steps you used.

Susan buys 16 packages of hot dogs for a barbecue. Each package contains 12 hot dogs. Hot dog buns are sold in packages of 8. How many packages of hot dog buns does Susan need to buy so she has one bun for each hot dog?

_____

Share Solutions

Use an equation to solve.

Show your work.

4 Admission to the theme park is $32 for each adult. A group of 5 adults and 1 child pays $182 to enter the theme park. How much is a child's ticket to the theme park?

_____

5 Kenny collects CDs and DVDs. He has a total of 208 CDs. He also has 8 shelves with 24 DVDs on each shelf. How many more CDs does Kenny have than DVDs?

_____

6 Carla plants 14 tomato plants. Her gardening book says that each plant should grow 12 tomatoes. She plans to divide the tomatoes equally among herself and 7 friends. How many tomatoes would each person get?

_____

7 Alex and his family go on a road trip. On the first day, they drive 228 miles. On the second day, they drive 279 miles. Their destination is 1,043 miles away. How many miles do they have left to drive to reach their destination?

_____

8 A public library has more than 50,000 books. There are 249 science books and 321 technology books. Mary sorts the science and technology books on shelves with 6 books on each shelf. How many shelves will Mary fill with science and technology books?

_____

✓ **Check Understanding**
Explain what two-step problems are and how to solve them.

Solve Two-Step Problems

Discuss the Steps

1 Mr. Stills makes bags of school supplies for the 9 students in his class. He has 108 pencils and 72 erasers. He puts the same number of pencils and the same number of erasers into each bag. How many more pencils than erasers are in each bag of school supplies?

Solve the problem by finishing Nicole's and David's methods. Discuss what is alike and what is different about the methods.

Nicole's Method

Write an equation for each step.

Divide to find the number of pencils that Mr. Stills puts in each bag of school supplies. $108 \div 9 =$ _____

Divide to find the number of erasers that Mr. Stills puts in each bag of school supplies. $72 \div 9 =$ _____

Subtract the number of erasers in each bag from the number of pencils in each bag. $12 - 8 =$ _____

There are _____ more pencils than erasers in each bag of school supplies.

David's Method

Write an equation for the whole problem.

Let $p =$ how many more pencils than erasers are in each bag of school supplies.

The number of pencils in each bag of school supplies

The number of erasers in each bag of school supplies

$$\text{\_\_\_\_} \div 9 - \text{\_\_\_\_} \div 9 = p$$
$$12 - 8 = p$$
$$\text{\_\_\_\_} = p$$

There are _____ more pencils than erasers in each bag of school supplies.

Discuss the Steps (continued)

2 John is selling bags of popcorn for a school fundraiser. So far, John has sold 45 bags of popcorn for $5 each. His goal is to earn $300 for the school fundraiser. How many more bags of popcorn must John sell to reach his goal?

Solve the problem by writing an equation for each step. Then solve the problem by writing one equation for the whole problem.

Write an equation for each step.

Multiply to find how much money John has earned so far selling popcorn.

$$\underline{\hspace{3em}} \times \quad \$5 \quad = \quad \$\underline{\hspace{3em}}$$

Subtract to find how much money John has left to earn to reach his goal.

$$\$300 \quad - \quad \$\underline{\hspace{3em}} \quad = \quad \$\underline{\hspace{3em}}$$

Divide to find the number of bags of popcorn John must sell to reach his goal.

$$\$75 \quad \div \quad \$5 \quad = \quad \underline{\hspace{3em}}$$

John must sell $\underline{\hspace{3em}}$ more bags of popcorn to reach his goal.

Write an equation for the whole problem.

Let b = the number of bags of popcorn John must sell to reach his goal.

John's fundraiser goal amount   Amount of money John has raised so far

$$(\underline{\hspace{3em}} \quad - \quad \underline{\hspace{3em}} \times \quad \$5) \quad \div \quad \$5 \quad = b$$

$$(\$300 \quad - \$\underline{\hspace{3em}}) \quad \div \quad \$5 \quad = b$$

$$\$\underline{\hspace{3em}} \quad \div \quad \$5 \quad = b$$

$$\underline{\hspace{3em}} \quad = b$$

John must sell $\underline{\hspace{3em}}$ more bags of popcorn to reach his goal.

Solve Multistep Problems

Multistep Word Problems

Use an equation to solve.

Show your work.

3 Sara bought some bags of beads. Each bag had 9 beads and cost $2. Sara used the beads to make 18 necklaces, each with 25 beads. How much money did Sara pay for the beads for all of the necklaces that she made?

_____

4 There are 5 fourth-grade classes going on a field trip. Two of the classes have 16 students each and 3 of the classes have 17 students each. They are travelling in vans that hold 9 students each. How many vans must they have to transport all the students?

_____

5 A movie theater has 13 screens. On weekends, each screen shows a movie 7 times in one day. On weekdays, each screen shows a movie 5 times in one day. How many more showings are there on Saturdays than on Tuesdays?

_____

6 Justin goes to the store and buys 3 T-shirts for $14 each. He also buys 2 pairs of jeans for $23 each. He gives the cashier $100. How much change does Justin receive?

_____

7 Terrence has 24 model cars arranged in equal rows of 6 model cars. Natalie has 18 model cars arranged in equal rows of 3 model cars. How many rows of model cars in all do they have?

_____

What's the Error?

Dear Math Students,

My friend and I are planning a hike. We will hike from Point A to Point B, which is a distance of 28 miles. Then we will hike from Point B to Point C, which is a distance of 34 miles. We will walk 7 miles each day for 8 days. We are trying to figure out how many miles we need to walk on the ninth day to reach Point C.

I wrote and solved this equation.

$28 + 34 - 7 \times 8 = t$

$62 - 7 \times 8 = t$

$55 \times 8 = t$

$440 = t$

This answer doesn't make sense. Did I do something wrong? What do you think?

Your friend,
Puzzled Penguin

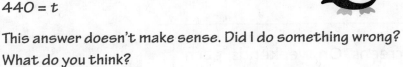

8 Write a response to Puzzled Penguin.

_____

_____

_____

_____

_____

_____

 Check Understanding

Describe how to solve a multistep problem.

Solve Multistep Problems

Name _____

Discuss Multistep Word Problems

Use equations to solve.

Show your work.

1. Eli reads 6 pages in a book each night. Shelby reads 8 pages each night. How many pages altogether will Eli and Shelby read in one week?

   _____

2. Min Soo is ordering 5 pizzas for a party. Each pizza will be cut into 8 slices. Three pizzas will have multiple toppings, and the others will be plain cheese. How many slices of plain cheese pizza is Min Soo ordering for the party?

   _____

3. Jasmine and Mori each received the same number of party favor bags last month. Each bag contained 8 favors. If Jasmine and Mori received a total of 48 favors, how many party favor bags did they each receive?

   _____

4. In art class, Ernesto made some fruit bowls for his mother and brother. Nine apples can be placed in each bowl. Ernesto's brother placed 18 apples in the bowls he was given, and Ernesto's mother placed 36 apples in the bowls she was given. How many fruit bowls did Ernesto make?

   _____

5. On Tuesday, a bicycle shop employee replaced all of the tires on 6 bicycles. On Wednesday, all of the tires on 5 tricycles were replaced. What is the total number of tires that were replaced on those days?

   _____

Solve Multistep Word Problems

Use equations to solve.

Show your work.

6 Mrs. Luong bought 9 trees for $40 each. She paid for her purchase with four $100 bills. How much change did she receive?

_____

7 The contents of Chan Hee's box weigh 37 pounds. In the box are five containers of equal weight, and a book that weighs 2 pounds. What is the weight of each container?

_____

8 A pet shop is home to 6 cats, 10 birds, 3 dogs, and 18 tropical fish. Altogether, how many legs do those pets have?

_____

9 Dan has 7 fish in his aquarium. Marilyn has 4 times as many fish in her aquarium. How many fish do Dan and Marilyn have altogether?

_____

10 Write a problem that is solved using more than one step. Then show how to solve the problem.

_____

_____

✓ **Check Understanding**

For Problem 7, suppose the contents of Chan Hee's box weigh 42 pounds. Write and solve a new equation to find the weight of each container.

_____

Practice with Multistep Problems

Write an equation to show the problem. Then solve.   *Show your work.*

1 Anika spent $128 on 3 sweaters and 1 skirt. The sweaters cost $38 each. What was the cost of the skirt?

_____

_____

2 Lily has 144 ceramic beads and 108 wooden beads. She plans to store the beads equally in 6 boxes. How many beads will be in each box?

_____

_____

Write one or more equations to show the problem. Then solve.

3 Emma has 14 rocks in her collection. Tyler has 6 times as many rocks as Emma. How many rocks do Emma and Tyler have altogether?

_____

_____

4 Joaquin is saving $250 to buy a surfboard. He saved $8 each week for 12 weeks. He wants to buy the surfboard in 7 more weeks. How much does Joaquin need to save each week?

_____

_____

Name _____ **Date** _____

Add or subtract.

1.
```
  60,047
- 35,689
```

2.
```
  472
- 364
```

3.
```
  5,682
+ 2,497
```

4.
```
  5,897
- 4,352
```

5.
```
  89,431
-  8,650
```

6.
```
  298
+ 311
```

7.
```
  67,538
+ 22,685
```

8.
```
  429
- 117
```

9.
```
  409,274
-  38,528
```

10.
```
  342
+ 342
```

11.
```
  5,630
- 3,428
```

12.
```
  587,390
+ 136,428
```

13.
```
  984,208
- 796,159
```

14.
```
  79,472
+  8,927
```

15.
```
  3,219
+   628
```

Name _____

Find Factor Pairs

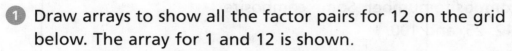

A factor pair for a number is two whole numbers whose product is that number. For example, 2 and 5 is a factor pair for 10.

1 Draw arrays to show all the factor pairs for 12 on the grid below. The array for 1 and 12 is shown.

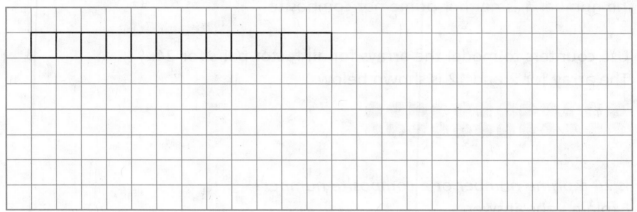

2 List all the factor pairs for 12. _____

Use the table to list all the factors pairs for each number.

3 32

1	32
2	

4 44

1	44

5 100

1	100

List all the factor pairs for each number.

6 29

_____

7 63

_____

Identify Prime and Composite Numbers

VOCABULARY
prime number
composite number

A number greater than 1 that has 1 and itself as its only factor pair is a **prime number**. Some prime numbers are 2, 5, 11, and 23.

A number greater than 1 that has more than one factor pair is a **composite number**. Some composite numbers are 4, 12, 25, and 100.

The number 1 is neither prime nor composite.

8 Use counters to model the arrays for all factor pairs for 24. The array for 2 and 12 is shown below.

9 Is 24 a *prime number* or a *composite number*? Explain your answer.

_____

_____

Write whether each number is *prime* or *composite*.

10 99

_____

11 72

_____

12 31

_____

13 45

_____

14 19

_____

15 88

_____

16 67

_____

17 100

_____

18 53

_____

19 Is 2 the only even prime number? Explain.

_____

_____

Factors and Multiples

VOCABULARY
multiple

A **multiple** of a number is a product of that number and a counting number.

20 What are the first five multiples of 4? Explain your method.

_____

_____

21 Write the first ten multiples of 8.

_____

22 Is 54 a multiple of 6? Explain how you know.

_____

_____

23 Is 6 a factor of 40? Explain how you know.

_____

24 What are the first five multiples of 9? Explain your method.

_____

_____

25 What are the factors of 63?

_____

26 Is 63 a multiple of each factor that you listed for Exercise 25? Explain how you know.

_____

_____

_____

Practice With Factors and Multiples

Tell whether 7 is a factor of each number. Write *yes* or *no*.

27 7 _____ **28** 84 _____ **29** 93 _____ **30** 49 _____

Tell whether each number is a multiple of 9. Write *yes* or *no*.

31 27 _____ **32** 30 _____ **33** 81 _____ **34** 99 _____

Use a pattern to find the unknown multiples.

35 $3 \times 11 = 33$

$4 \times 11 = 44$

$5 \times 11 =$ _____

$6 \times 11 =$ _____

$7 \times 11 =$ _____

36 $5 \times 6 = 30$

$6 \times 6 =$ _____

$7 \times 6 =$ _____

$8 \times 6 =$ _____

$9 \times 6 =$ _____

Use the rule to complete the pattern.

37 Rule: skip count by 6

6, _____, _____, 24, _____, 36, _____, 48, _____, 60

38 Rule: skip count by 5

5, 10, _____, 20, 25, _____, 35, 40, _____, _____, 55, _____

39 Rule: skip count by 7

7, 14, 21, _____, _____, _____, _____, _____, _____, _____

40 Rule: skip count by 12

12, 24, _____, _____, _____, _____, _____, _____, _____

✓ **Check Understanding**

Draw arrays for the factor pairs for 18. Is 18 a prime number

or a composite number? _____

Factors and Prime Numbers

Name _____

Numerical Patterns

A **pattern** is a sequence that can be described by a rule.

Use the rule to find the next three terms in the pattern.

1 22, 24, 26, 28, 30, …
Rule: add 2

_____

2 5, 10, 20, 40, …
Rule: multiply by 2

_____

3 1, 3, 9, 27, …
Rule: multiply by 3

_____

4 2, 9, 16, 23, 30, …
Rule: add 7

_____

Use the rule to find the first ten terms in the pattern.

5 First term: 9   Rule: add 5

_____

6 First term: 10   Rule: add 60

_____

Real World Applications

Solve.

7 Amy lives in the twentieth house on Elm Street. The first house on Elm Street is numbered 3. The second is 6. The third is 9. The fourth is 12. If this pattern continues, what is Amy's house number likely to be?

House	1st	2nd	3rd	4th	20th
Number	3	6	9	12	

_____

8 Theo runs 5 miles every morning. He tracks his progress on a chart to log how many miles he has run in all. How many miles will Theo write on day 100?

Day	1	2	3	4	5	100
Miles	5	10	15	20	25	

_____

Extend Patterns

9 What are the repeating terms of the pattern?

_____

10 What will be the tenth term in the pattern? _____

11 What will be the fifteenth term in the pattern? _____

Growing Patterns

12 How does each figure in the pattern at the right change from one term to the next?

_____

_____

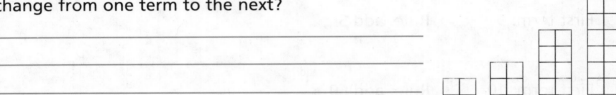

13 Describe the number of squares in the next term in the pattern of squares.

_____

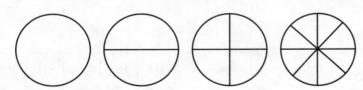

14 How does each figure in the pattern above change from one term to the next?

_____

15 How many equal parts will be in the seventh term?

_____

✓ Check Understanding

Use the rule to write the first five terms in the pattern.
First term: 8; Rule: multiply by 4

_____

Analyze Patterns

Math and Pottery

Pottery are objects that are first shaped of wet clay and then hardened by baking. Four steps are needed to make a pottery product: preparing the clay mixture, shaping the clay, decorating and glazing the product, and baking the product. Pottery includes products such as works of art, dinnerware, vases, and other household items. Some of the places you can find pottery include art studios, crafts shows, pottery stores, and many households.

Write an equation to solve.   *Show your work.*

1 A small pottery store has 9 same-size boxes full of pottery items. The boxes weigh 765 pounds in all. How much does each box weigh?

_____

2 Julio and Myra had a pottery stand at the annual craft fair. They sold some of their pottery at the original price of $13 each and made $780. Later in the day, they decreased the price of each item by $4 and sold 20 more items. How much money did they make in all that day?

_____

© Houghton Mifflin Harcourt Publishing Company • Image Credits: ©Image Source/Getty Images

Content Standards **4.OA.A.1, 4.OA.A.2, 4.OA.A.3, 4.OA.C.5, 4.NBT.B.4, 4.NBT.B.5, 4.NBT.B.6, 4.MD.A.2**
Mathematical Practices MP1, MP3, MP4, MP5, MP6, MP7, MP8

Focus on Mathematical Practices **197**

Write an equation to solve.

Show your work.

3 Last month, Mr. Smith bought 65 small cans of paint for his pottery shop. This month he bought 3 times as many small cans of paint. How many small cans of paint did he buy this month?

_____

4 The employees at a pottery warehouse are packing boxes of vases to be delivered by truck. They packed 824 small vases in boxes that each hold 8 vases. They also packed 296 large vases in boxes that each hold 4 vases. How many boxes did the workers pack in all?

_____

5 Last year, there were 3,875 different pottery items for sale at a large crafts show. This year, there were 1,260 fewer pottery items for sale at the crafts show. How many pottery items were for sale at the crafts show this year?

_____

Solve.

6 Isabella saw a pottery design that she liked at a crafts store. She wants to copy the design and paint it on a pot she is making. Part of the design is shown below.

a. What shape should Isabella paint next to continue the design's pattern?

_____

b. What will be the fourteenth shape in Isabella's design?

_____

Focus on Mathematical Practices

Write whether the number is *prime* or *composite*.

1 91

_____

2 41

_____

3 List all factor pairs for the number.

64

_____

4 Use the rule to find the next three terms in the pattern.

4, 12, 36, 108, ...
Rule: multiply by 3

_____

5 Describe the next term in the pattern.

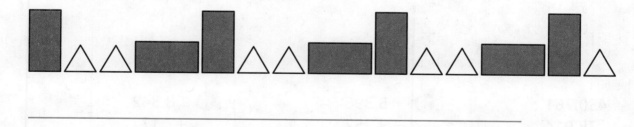

_____

_____

Name _____ **Date** _____

Add or subtract.

1
```
  24,389
+ 18,710
```

2
```
  506
− 382
```

3
```
  5,537
+ 4,548
```

4
```
  637
+ 462
```

5
```
  43,000
−  6,782
```

6
```
  52,896
− 36,952
```

7
```
  11,934
+  4,572
```

8
```
  692,375
+ 227,964
```

9
```
  353,785
− 177,841
```

10
```
  409
+ 570
```

11
```
  4,507
− 3,384
```

12
```
  755
− 314
```

13
```
  430,761
−  78,914
```

14
```
  5,396
− 3,352
```

15
```
  8,342
+  177
```

1 The number of ash trees on a tree farm is 5 times the number of pine trees. Choose one expression from each column to create an equation that compares the number of ash trees (*a*) and pine trees (*p*).

○ $a - 5$	○ p
○ $5a$	○ $5p$
○ a	○ $p + 5$
○ $a \div 5$	○ $p - 5$

= (between the two columns)

2 Katie canned 182 quarts of tomatoes last week. She canned 259 quarts of tomatoes this week. How many quarts of tomatoes (*q*) did Katie can over these two weeks? Write an equation. Then solve.

Equation: _____

$q =$ _____ quarts

3 Eliot sends 217 text messages each week. Write equations to find how many text messages he sends in 4 weeks and in 7 weeks.

Equations: _____

_____

Use the equations to complete the table.

Weeks	Total Text Messages
1	217
4	
7	

4 Solve for *n*.

$(16 + 12) \div (11 - 7) = n$ $n =$ ☐

5 There are 1,342 players in the baseball league. That is
2 times the number of players in the football league.
How many players are in the football league? Write an
equation. Then solve.

6 A school ordered 688 T-shirts in 3 sizes: small, medium,
and large. There are 296 small and 268 medium T-shirts.
How many large T-shirts were ordered? Select numbers
from the list to complete the equation. Then solve.

3   268   296   688

$l = \boxed{} - \left(\boxed{} + \boxed{} \right)$

$l =$ _____ large T-shirts

7 Select the factor pair for 45. Mark all that apply.

(A) 4, 11   (C) 6, 7   (E) 1, 45

(B) 3, 15   (D) 4, 12   (F) 5, 9

8 Is a multiple of the prime number 3 also a prime
number? Circle your answer.

Yes   No

Explain your reasoning.

9 For Exercises 9a–9e, choose Yes or No to tell whether the number is prime.

9a. 49　　　　　　　○ Yes　　○ No

9b. 53　　　　　　　○ Yes　　○ No

9c. 63　　　　　　　○ Yes　　○ No

9d. 37　　　　　　　○ Yes　　○ No

9e. 51　　　　　　　○ Yes　　○ No

10 Classify each number from the list as being a multiple of 2, 3, or 5. Write each number in the correct box. A number can be written in more than one box.

| 18 | 30 | 20 | 24 | 55 | 39 |

Multiple of 2	**Multiple of 3**	**Multiple of 5**

11 Use the rule to find the next 3 terms in the pattern.

Rule: multiply by 2

4, 8, 16, 32, ☐ , ☐ , ☐ , …

12 Draw the next term in the pattern.

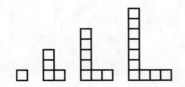

13 A team of workers is building a 942-foot trail. They plan to complete 6 feet per hour. How many hours will it take to build the trail?

Choose the equation that can be used to solve this problem. Mark all that apply.

(A) $942 \times 6 = h$ (D) $6 \times h = 942$

(B) $942 \div 6 = h$ (E) $6 = 942 \times h$

(C) $942 \div h = 6$ (F) $942 = 6 \div h$

14 Roger ships a large number of packages on Monday. Then he ships 3,820 more packages on Tuesday. Roger ships 22,540 packages in all. How many packages did he ship on Monday? Identify the type of comparison as addition or multiplication. Then write and solve an equation to solve the problem.

Type of comparison: _____

Equation: _____

Answer: _____ packages

15 For Exercises 15a–15d, select True or False for the calculation.

15a. $72 \div (6 + 2) = 9$ ○ True ○ False

15b. $(2 + 7) + (6 - 2) = 36$ ○ True ○ False

15c. $(12 + 8) \div 4 = 10 \div (5 - 3)$ ○ True ○ False

15d. $(35 - 8) \div (2 + 1) = 32$ ○ True ○ False

16 Charlotte made this pictograph to show the number of dogs attending a dog training class this week.

Dogs in Training Class

Monday	🐾 🐾 🐾
Wednesday	🐾 🐾
Friday	🐾 🐾 🐾 🐾 🐾 🐾 🐾
Saturday	🐾 🐾 🐾 🐾 🐾 🐾 🐾 🐾

🐾 = 3 dogs

Part A

How many fewer dogs were in training class on Monday than on Friday? Write and solve an equation.

Equation: _____

Answer: _____ fewer dogs

Part B

Choose the number that makes the sentence true.

Charlotte forgot to include Thursday on her graph. There were two times as many dogs at Thursday's class than at Monday's class.

There were | 2 / 6 / 15 / 18 | dogs in the training class on Thursday.

Part C

Explain how you determined the number of dogs at Thursday's class.

17 The Ruiz family bought 2 adult tickets and 4 child tickets to the fair. The adult tickets cost $8 each. The child tickets cost $3 each.

Part A
Complete the equation Zach and Alannah wrote to find the total cost of the tickets bought by the Ruiz family.

$$\left(\boxed{} \times \boxed{} \right) + \left(4 \times \boxed{} \right) = c$$

Part B
Zach's answer is $72, and Alannah's answer is $28. Who has the wrong answer? Explain what error he or she made.

18 A store has 4 bins of planet posters with 23 posters in each bin. It has 3 bins of planet calendars with 26 calendars in each bin. Yesterday, 72 calendars were sold. How many planet posters and calendars are left in all? Explain how you found your answer, and how you know if your answer is reasonable.

Find Their Ages

Tricia, Molly, and Becky are cousins. At a family reunion, their Aunt Sasha makes it a game for the other relatives to find the age of each cousin. Aunt Sasha tells the relatives that Becky is 2 years older than Molly. She says that Tricia's age is 3 times Molly's age right now.

1 Write an equation relating Becky's age to Molly's age.

_____

2 Write an equation relating Tricia's age to Molly's age.

_____

3 If Molly is 3, how old is Becky? Show your work.

_____

_____

4 How old is Tricia? Show your work.

_____

_____

5 Write an equation that relates Tricia's age to Becky's age. Show that your equation is true.

_____

_____

_____

_____

James, Ben, and David are cousins who are also at the family reunion. James is 12 years old, Ben is 16 years old, and David is 18 years old. The cousins decide to play a game for the other relatives to find the ages of their uncles.

6 The cousins said that Uncle Reggie is twice as many years old as James' and Ben's ages together. Use one or more equations to find out how old Uncle Reggie is. Show your work.

_____

_____

7 Then the cousins said that Uncle Tony is 4 years younger than 3 times David's age. Use one or more equations to find out how old Uncle Tony is. Show your work.

_____

_____

8 The cousins also said that Uncle Ed is half as old as all of their ages combined. Use one or more equations to find out how old Uncle Ed is. Show your work.

_____

_____

9 Write and solve an equation relating your age to the age of someone in your family. Use at least one variable. Explain how you wrote the equation.

_____

_____

_____

Examples of Metric Units

Length

1 kilometer (km)	1 hectometer (hm)	1 dekameter (dam)	1 meter (m)
about the distance you could walk in 12 minutes 1 km = 1,000 m	about the length of a football field 1 hm = 100 m	about the length of a school bus 1 dam = 10 m	about the distance from the floor to the doorknob

1 decimeter (dm)	1 centimeter (cm)	1 millimeter (mm)
about the length of a new crayon 10 dm = 1 m	about the width of your finger 100 cm = 1 m	about the thickness of a dime 1,000 mm = 1 m

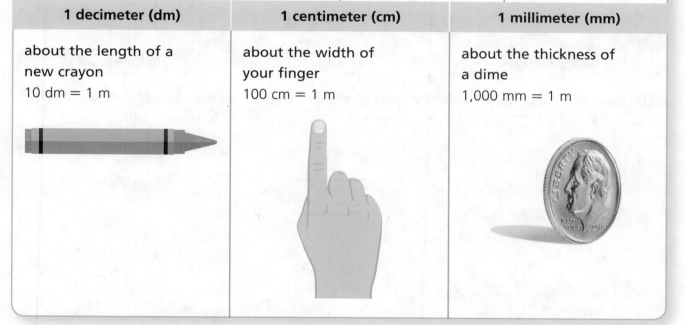

Metric Units

Examples of Metric Units

Liquid Volume

1 kiloliter (kL)	1 liter (L)	1 milliliter (mL)
This cube holds 1 kiloliter of liquid. 1 kL = 1,000 L 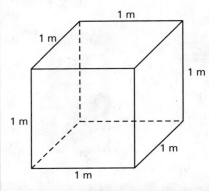	This cube holds 1 liter of liquid. 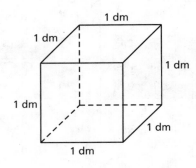	This cube holds 1 milliliter of liquid. 1,000 mL = 1 L 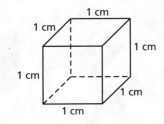

Mass

1 kilogram (kg)	1 gram (g)	1 milligram (mg)
The mass of 5 bananas is about 1 kilogram. 1 kg = 1,000 g 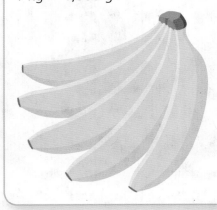	The mass of a paper clip is about 1 gram. 	The mass of a pinch of salt is about 1 milligram. 1,000 mg = 1 g 

Examples of Customary Units

Length

1 inch (in.)	1 foot (ft)	1 yard (yd)	1 mile (mi)
The distance across a quarter is about 1 inch.	The length of your math book is about 1 foot. 1 ft = 12 in.	The length of a guitar is about 1 yard. 1 yd = 3 ft	You can walk 1 mile in about 20 minutes. 1 mi = 5,280 ft = 1,760 yd

Liquid Volume

1 cup (c)	1 pint (pt)	1 quart (qt)
1 c = 8 fluid ounces	1 pt = 2 c	1 qt = 2 pt = 4 c

1 half gallon ($\frac{1}{2}$ gal)	1 gallon (gal)
$\frac{1}{2}$ gal = 2 qt	1 gal = 4 qt

Customary Units

Examples of Customary Units

Weight

1 ounce (oz)	1 pound (lb)	1 ton (T)
A slice of bread weighs about 1 ounce.	A package of butter weighs 1 pound. 1 lb = 16 oz	A small car weighs about 1 ton. 1 T = 2,000 lb

Table of Measures

Metric	Customary

Length/Area

Metric	Customary
1,000 millimeters (mm) = 1 meter (m)	1 foot (ft) = 12 inches (in.)
100 centimeters (cm) = 1 meter	1 yard (yd) = 36 inches
10 decimeters (dm) = 1 meter	1 yard = 3 feet
1 dekameter (dam) = 10 meters	1 mile (mi) = 5,280 feet
1 hectometer (hm) = 100 meters	1 mile = 1,760 yards
1 kilometer (km) = 1,000 meters	

Liquid Volume

Metric	Customary
1,000 milliliters (mL) = 1 liter (L)	6 teaspoons (tsp) = 1 fluid ounce (fl oz)
100 centiliters (cL) = 1 liter	2 tablespoons (tbsp) = 1 fluid ounce
10 deciliters (dL) = 1 liter	1 cup (c) = 8 fluid ounces
1 dekaliter (daL) = 10 liters	1 pint (pt) = 2 cups
1 hectoliter (hL) = 100 liters	1 quart (qt) = 2 pints
1 kiloliter (kL) = 1,000 liters	1 gallon (gal) = 4 quarts

Mass / Weight

Mass	Weight
1,000 milligrams (mg) = 1 gram (g)	1 pound (lb) = 16 ounces
100 centigrams (cg) = 1 gram	1 ton (T) = 2,000 pounds
10 decigrams (dg) = 1 gram	
1 dekagram (dag) = 10 grams	
1 hectogram (hg) = 100 grams	
1 kilogram (kg) = 1,000 grams	
1 metric ton = 1,000 kilograms	

Reference Tables

Table of Units of Time

Time

1 minute (min) = 60 seconds (sec)	1 year = 365 days
1 hour (hr) = 60 minutes	1 leap year = 366 days
1 day = 24 hours	1 decade = 10 years
1 week (wk) = 7 days	1 century = 100 years
1 month is about 30 days	1 millennium = 1,000 years
1 year (yr) = 12 months (mo) or about 52 weeks	

Table of Formulas

Perimeter

Polygon

P = sum of the lengths of the sides

Rectangle

$P = 2(l + w)$ or $P = 2l + 2w$

Square

$P = 4s$

Area

Rectangle

$A = lw$ or $A = bh$

Square

$A = s \cdot s$

Properties of Operations

Associative Property of Addition

$(a + b) + c = a + (b + c)$	$(2 + 5) + 3 = 2 + (5 + 3)$

Commutative Property of Addition

$a + b = b + a$	$4 + 6 = 6 + 4$

Addition Identity Property of 0

$a + 0 = 0 + a = a$	$3 + 0 = 0 + 3 = 3$

Associative Property of Multiplication

$(a \cdot b) \cdot c = a \cdot (b \cdot c)$	$(3 \cdot 5) \cdot 7 = 3 \cdot (5 \cdot 7)$

Commutative Property of Multiplication

$a \cdot b = b \cdot a$	$6 \cdot 3 = 3 \cdot 6$

Multiplicative Identity Property of 1

$a \cdot 1 = 1 \cdot a = a$	$8 \cdot 1 = 1 \cdot 8 = 8$

Distributive Property of Multiplication over Addition

$a \cdot (b + c) = (a \cdot b) + (a \cdot c)$	$2 \cdot (4 + 3) = (2 \cdot 4) + (2 \cdot 3)$

Addition and Subtraction Problem Types

	Result Unknown	Change Unknown	Start Unknown
Add to	A glass contained $\frac{3}{4}$ cup of orange juice. Then $\frac{1}{4}$ cup of pineapple juice was added. How much juice is in the glass now? *Situation and solution equation:* [1] $\frac{3}{4} + \frac{1}{4} = c$	A glass contained $\frac{3}{4}$ cup of orange juice. Then some pineapple juice was added. Now the glass contains 1 cup of juice. How much pineapple juice was added? *Situation equation:* $\frac{3}{4} + c = 1$ *Solution equation:* $c = 1 - \frac{3}{4}$	A glass contained some orange juice. Then $\frac{1}{4}$ cup of pineapple juice was added. Now the glass contains 1 cup of juice. How much orange juice was in the glass to start? *Situation equation:* $c + \frac{1}{4} = 1$ *Solution equation:* $c = 1 - \frac{1}{4}$
Take from	Micah had a ribbon $\frac{5}{6}$ yard long. He cut off a piece $\frac{1}{6}$ yard long. What is the length of the ribbon that is left? *Situation and solution equation:* $\frac{5}{6} - \frac{1}{6} = r$	Micah had a ribbon $\frac{5}{6}$ yard long. He cut off a piece. Now the ribbon is $\frac{4}{6}$ yard long. What is the length of the ribbon he cut off? *Situation equation:* $\frac{5}{6} - r = \frac{4}{6}$ *Solution equation:* $r = \frac{5}{6} - \frac{4}{6}$	Micah had a ribbon. He cut off a piece $\frac{1}{6}$ yard long. Now the ribbon is $\frac{4}{6}$ yard long. What was the length of the ribbon he started with? *Situation equation:* $r - \frac{1}{6} = \frac{4}{6}$ *Solution equation:* $r = \frac{4}{6} + \frac{1}{6}$

[1] A situation equation represents the structure (action) in the problem situation. A solution equation shows the operation used to find the answer.

Addition and Subtraction Problem Types (continued)

	Total Unknown	Addend Unknown	Other Addend Unknown
Put Together/ Take Apart	A baker combines $1\frac{2}{3}$ cups of white flour and $\frac{2}{3}$ cup of wheat flour. How much flour is this altogether? *Math drawing:*[1] f $1\frac{2}{3}$ $\frac{2}{3}$ *Situation and solution equation:* $1\frac{2}{3} + \frac{2}{3} = f$	Of the $2\frac{1}{3}$ cups of flour a baker uses, $1\frac{2}{3}$ cups are white flour. The rest is wheat flour. How much wheat flour does the baker use? *Math drawing:* $2\frac{1}{3}$ $1\frac{2}{3}$ f *Situation equation:* $2\frac{1}{3} = 1\frac{2}{3} + f$ *Solution equation:* $f = 2\frac{1}{3} - 1\frac{2}{3}$	A baker uses $2\frac{1}{3}$ cups of flour. Some is white flour and $\frac{2}{3}$ cup is wheat flour. How much white flour does the baker use? *Math drawing:* $2\frac{1}{3}$ f $\frac{2}{3}$ *Situation equation:* $2\frac{1}{3} = f + \frac{2}{3}$ *Solution equation:* $f = 2\frac{1}{3} - \frac{2}{3}$

Both Addends Unknown is a productive extension of this basic situation, especially for finding two fractions with a sum of 1. Such take apart situations can be used to show all the decompositions of a given number. The associated equations, which have the total on the left of the equal sign, help students understand that the = sign does not always mean *makes* or *results in* but always does mean *is the same number as.*

Both Addends Unknown

A baker is making different kinds of bread using only the $\frac{1}{4}$ cup measure. What different mixtures can be made with white flour and wheat flour to total 1 cup?

Math drawing:

1
a b

Situation equation:
$1 = a + b$

[1]These math drawings are called math mountains in Grades 1–3 and break apart drawings in Grades 4 and 5.

© Houghton Mifflin Harcourt Publishing Company

Problem Types

Addition and Subtraction Problem Types (continued)

	Difference Unknown	Greater Unknown	Smaller Unknown
Additive Comparison[1]	At a zoo, the female rhino weighs $1\frac{3}{5}$ tons. The male rhino weighs $2\frac{2}{5}$ tons. How much more does the male rhino weigh than the female rhino? At a zoo, the female rhino weighs $1\frac{3}{5}$ tons. The male rhino weighs $2\frac{2}{5}$ tons. How much less does the female rhino weigh than the male rhino? *Math drawing:* $2\frac{2}{5}$ $1\frac{3}{5}$　d *Situation equation:* $1\frac{3}{5} + d = 2\frac{2}{5}$　or $d = 2\frac{2}{5} - 1\frac{3}{5}$ *Solution equation:* $d = 2\frac{2}{5} - 1\frac{3}{5}$	**Leading Language** At a zoo, the female rhino weighs $1\frac{3}{5}$ tons. The male rhino weighs $\frac{4}{5}$ ton more than the female rhino. How much does the male rhino weigh? **Misleading Language** At a zoo, the female rhino weighs $1\frac{3}{5}$ tons. The female rhino weighs $\frac{4}{5}$ ton less than the male rhino. How much does the male rhino weigh? *Math drawing:* m $1\frac{3}{5}$　$\frac{4}{5}$ *Situation and solution equation:* $1\frac{3}{5} + \frac{4}{5} = m$	**Leading Language** At a zoo, the male rhino weighs $2\frac{2}{5}$ tons. The female rhino weighs $\frac{4}{5}$ ton less than the male rhino. How much does the female rhino weigh? **Misleading Language** At a zoo, the male rhino weighs $2\frac{2}{5}$ tons. The male rhino weighs $\frac{4}{5}$ ton more than the female rhino. How much does the female rhino weigh? *Math drawing:* $2\frac{2}{5}$ f　$\frac{4}{5}$ *Situation equation:* $f + \frac{4}{5} = 2\frac{2}{5}$　or $f = 2\frac{2}{5} - \frac{4}{5}$ *Solution equation:* $f = 2\frac{2}{5} - \frac{4}{5}$

[1]A comparison sentence can always be said in two ways. One way uses *more*, and the other uses *fewer* or *less*. Misleading language suggests the wrong operation. For example, it says *the female rhino weighs $\frac{4}{5}$ ton less than the male*, but you have to add $\frac{4}{5}$ ton to the female's weight to get the male's weight.

Multiplication and Division Problem Types

	Product Unknown	Group Size Unknown	Number of Groups Unknown
Equal Groups	A teacher bought 10 boxes of pencils. There are 20 pencils in each box. How many pencils did the teacher buy? *Situation and solution equation:* $p = 10 \cdot 20$	A teacher bought 10 boxes of pencils. She bought 200 pencils in all. How many pencils are in each box? *Situation equation:* $10 \cdot n = 200$ *Solution equation:* $n = 200 \div 10$	A teacher bought boxes of 20 pencils. She bought 200 pencils in all. How many boxes of pencils did she buy *Situation equation:* $b \cdot 20 = 200$ *Solution equation:* $b = 200 \div 20$

	Product Unknown	Factor Unknown	Factor Unknown
Arrays[1]	An auditorium has 60 rows with 30 seats in each row. How many seats are in the auditorium? *Math drawing:* 30 60 $\boxed{s}$ *Situation and solution equation:* $s = 60 \cdot 30$	An auditorium has 60 rows with the same number of seats in each row. There are 1,800 seats in all. How many seats are in each row? *Math drawing:* n 60 $\boxed{1{,}800}$ *Situation equation:* $60 \cdot n = 1{,}800$ *Solution equation:* $n = 1{,}800 \div 60$	The 1,800 seats in an auditorium are arranged in rows of 30. How many rows of seats are there? *Math drawing:* 30 r $\boxed{1{,}800}$ *Situation equation:* $r \cdot 30 = 1{,}800$ *Solution equation:* $r = 1{,}800 \div 30$

[1]We use rectangle models for both array and area problems in Grades 4 and 5 because the numbers in the problems are too large to represent with arrays.

Problem Types

Multiplication and Division Problem Types (continued)

	Product Unknown	Factor Unknown	Factor Unknown
Area	Sophie's backyard is 80 feet long and 40 feet wide. What is the area of Sophie's backyard? Math drawing: 80 40 A Situation and solution equation: $A = 80 \cdot 40$	Sophie's backyard has an area of 3,200 square feet. The length of the yard is 80 feet. What is the width of the yard? Math drawing: 80 w 3,200 Situation equation: $80 \cdot w = 3,200$ Solution equation: $w = 3,200 \div 80$	Sophie's backyard has an area of 3,200 square feet. The width of the yard is 40 feet. What is the length of the yard? Math drawing: l 40 3,200 Situation equation: $l \cdot 40 = 3,200$ Solution equation: $l = 3,200 \div 40$
Multiplicative Comparison	**Multiplier 1: Larger Unknown** Sam has 4 times as many marbles as Brady has. Brady has 70 marbles. How many marbles does Sam have? Math drawing: s | 70 | 70 | 70 | 70 | b | 70 | $b = s \div 4$ and $s = 4 \cdot b$ Situation and solution equation: $s = 4 \cdot 70$	**Multiplier 1: Smaller Unknown** Sam has 4 times as many marbles as Brady has. Sam has 280 marbles. How many marbles does Brady have? Math drawing: 280 s b $b = s \div 4$ and $s = 4 \cdot b$ Situation equation: $4 \cdot b = 280$ Situation and solution equation: $b = 280 \div 4$	**Multiplier 1: Unknown** Sam has 280 marbles. Brady has 70 marbles. The number of marbles Sam has is how many times the number Brady has? Math drawing: 280 s | 70 | 70 | 70 | 70 | b | 70 | $m \cdot b = s$ Situation equation: $m \cdot 70 = 280$ Solution equation: $m = 280 \div 70$

MathWord **Power**

Word Review

Work with a partner. Choose a word from the current unit or a review word from a previous unit. Use the word to complete one of the activities listed on the right. Then ask your partner if they have any edits to your work or questions about what you described. Repeat, having your partner choose a word.

Crossword Puzzle

Create a crossword puzzle similar to the example below. Use vocabulary words from the unit. You can add other related words, too. Challenge your partner to solve the puzzle.

Activities

* Give the meaning in words or gestures.
* Use the word in a sentence.
* Give another word that is related to the word in some way and explain the relationship.

Across

2. The answer to an addition problem
4. _____ and subtraction are inverse operations.
5. To put amounts together
6. When you trade 10 ones for 1 ten, you _____.

Down

1. The number to be divided in a division problem
2. The operation that you can use to find out how much more one number is than another.
3. A fraction with a numerator of 1 is a _____ fraction.

Vocabulary Activities

Word Wall

With your teacher's permission, start a word wall in your classroom. As you work through each lesson, put the math vocabulary words on index cards and place them on the word wall. You can work with a partner or a small group choosing a word and giving the definition.

Word Web

Make a word web for a word or words you do not understand in a unit. Fill in the web with words or phrases that are related to the vocabulary word.

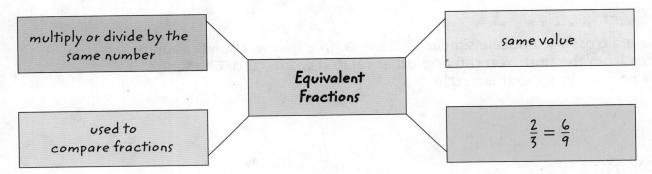

multiply or divide by the same number

used to compare fractions

Equivalent Fractions

same value

$$\frac{2}{3} = \frac{6}{9}$$

Alphabet Challenge

Take an alphabet challenge. Choose 3 letters from the alphabet. Think of three vocabulary words for each letter. Then write the definition or draw an example for each word.

A
addition
Associative Property
area

E
equation
expanded form
estimate

L
liter
line
line plot

Concentration

Write the vocabulary words and related words from a unit on index cards. Write the definitions on a different set of index cards. Choose 3 to 6 pairs of vocabulary words and definitions. Mix up the set of pairs. Then place the cards facedown on a table. Take turns turning over two cards. If one card is a word and one card is a definition that matches the word, take the pair. Continue until each word has been matched with its definition.

area

The number of square units that cover a figure.

Math Journal

As you learn new words, write them in your Math Journal. Write the definition of the word and include a sketch or an example. As you learn new information about the word, add notes to your definition.

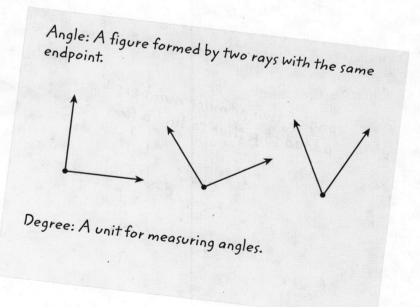

Angle: A figure formed by two rays with the same endpoint.

Degree: A unit for measuring angles.

What's the Word?

Work together to make a poster or bulletin board display of the words in a unit. Write definitions on a set of index cards. Mix up the cards. Work with a partner, choosing a definition from the index cards. Have your partner point to the word on the poster and name the matching math vocabulary word. Switch roles and try the activity again.

array

place value

addend

inverse operations

expanded form

word form

standard form

digit

one of two or more numbers added together to find a sum

A

acute angle
An angle smaller than a right angle.

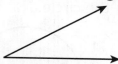

acute triangle
A triangle with three acute angles.

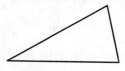

addend
One of two or more numbers added together to find a sum.

Example:

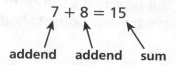

$$7 + 8 = 15$$

addend   addend   sum

adjacent sides
Two sides that meet at a point.

Example:
Sides *a* and *b* are adjacent.

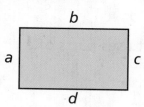

Algebraic Notation Method*
A strategy based on the Distributive Property in which a factor is decomposed to create simpler algebraic expressions, and the Distributive Property is applied.

Example:
$9 \cdot 28 = 9 \cdot (20 + 8)$
$\qquad = (9 \cdot 20) + (9 \cdot 8)$
$\qquad = 180 + 72$
$\qquad = 252$

analog clock
A clock with a face and hands.

angle
A figure formed by two rays with the same endpoint.

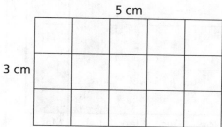

area
The number of square units that cover a figure.

array
An arrangement of objects, symbols, or numbers in rows and columns.

Associative Property of Addition
Grouping the addends in different ways does not change the sum.

Example:
$3 + (5 + 7) = 15$
$(3 + 5) + 7 = 15$

*A classroom research-based term developed for *Math Expressions*

Glossary

Associative Property of Multiplication
Grouping the factors in different ways does not change the product.

Example:
$3 \times (5 \times 7) = 105$
$(3 \times 5) \times 7 = 105$

bar graph
A graph that uses bars to show data. The bars may be vertical or horizontal.

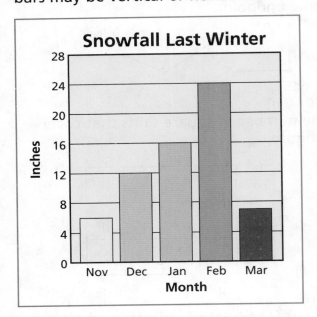

Snowfall Last Winter

break-apart drawing*
A diagram that shows two addends and the sum.

center
The point that is the same distance from every point on the circle.

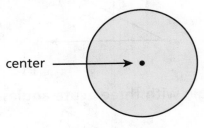

center

centimeter (cm)
A unit of measure in the metric system that equals one hundredth of a meter.
100 cm = 1 m

circle
A plane figure that forms a closed path so that all the points on the path are the same distance from a point called the center.

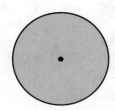

circle graph
A graph that uses parts of a circle to show data.

Example:

Favorite Fiction Books

Humor

Fantasy

Adventure

Mystery

© Houghton Mifflin Harcourt Publishing Company

*A classroom research-based term developed for *Math Expressions*

column

A part of a table or array that contains items arranged vertically.

● ● ● ●
● ● ● ●
● ● ● ●
● ● ● ●

common denominator

A common multiple of two or more denominators.

Example:
A common denominator of $\frac{1}{2}$ and $\frac{1}{3}$ is 6 because 6 is a multiple of 2 and 3.

Commutative Property of Addition

Changing the order of addends does not change the sum.

Example: $3 + 8 = 11$
$8 + 3 = 11$

Commutative Property of Multiplication

Changing the order of factors does not change the product.

Example: $3 \times 8 = 24$
$8 \times 3 = 24$

compare

Describe quantities as greater than, less than, or equal to each other.

comparison bars*

Bars that represent the larger amount and smaller amount in a comparison situation.

For addition and subtraction:

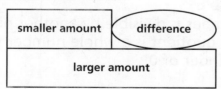

For multiplication and division:

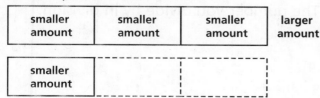

comparison situation*

A situation in which two amounts are compared by addition or by multiplication. An *addition comparison situation* compares by asking or telling how much more (how much less) one amount is than another. A *multiplication comparison situation* compares by asking or telling how many times as many one amount is as another. The multiplication comparison may also be made using fraction language. For example, you can say, "Sally has one fourth as much as Tom has," instead of saying "Tom has 4 times as much as Sally has."

composite number

A number greater than 1 that has more than one factor pair. Examples of composite numbers are 10 and 18. The factor pairs of 10 are 1 and 10, 2 and 5. The factor pairs of 18 are 1 and 18, 2 and 9, 3 and 6.

cup (c)

A unit of liquid volume in the customary system that equals 8 fluid ounces.

D

data

A collection of information.

decimal number

A representation of a number using the numerals 0 to 9, in which each digit has a value 10 times the digit to its right. A dot or **decimal point** separates the whole-number part of the number on the left from the fractional part on the right.

Examples:
1.23 and 0.3

*A classroom research-based term developed for *Math Expressions*

decimal point

A symbol used to separate dollars and cents in money amounts or to separate ones and tenths in decimal numbers.

Examples:

$8.59   1.2
↑   ↑
decimal point

decimeter (dm)

A unit of measure in the metric system that equals one tenth of a meter.
10 dm = 1 m

degree (°)

A unit for measuring angles.

denominator

The number below the bar in a fraction. It shows the total number of equal parts in the whole.

Example:

$\frac{3}{4}$ ← **denominator**

diagonal of a quadrilateral

A line segment that connects two opposite corners (vertices).

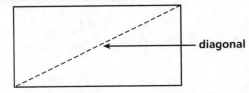
diagonal

difference

The result of a subtraction.

Example:
54 − 37 = 17 ← difference

digit

Any of the symbols 0, 1, 2, 3, 4, 5, 6, 7, 8, or 9.

digital clock

A clock that shows us the hour and minutes with numbers.

Digit-by-Digit*

A method used to solve a division problem.

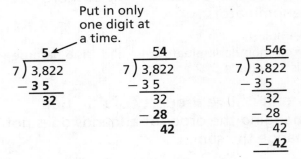

Put in only one digit at a time.

$$5$$
$$7\overline{)3{,}822}$$
$$-3\,5$$
$$\overline{32}$$

$$54$$
$$7\overline{)3{,}822}$$
$$-3\,5$$
$$\overline{32}$$
$$-28$$
$$\overline{42}$$

$$546$$
$$7\overline{)3{,}822}$$
$$-3\,5$$
$$\overline{32}$$
$$-28$$
$$\overline{42}$$
$$-42$$

Distributive Property

You can multiply a sum by a number, or multiply each addend by the number and add the products; the result is the same.

Example:
$3 \times (2 + 4) = (3 \times 2) + (3 \times 4)$
$3 \times 6 \quad = \quad 6 \quad + \quad 12$
$18 \quad = \quad 18$

dividend

The number that is divided in division.

Example:

$\frac{7}{9\overline{)63}}$

63 is the dividend.

divisible

A number is divisible by another number if the quotient is a whole number with a remainder of 0.

divisor

The number you divide by in division.

Example:

$\frac{7}{9\overline{)63}}$

9 is the divisor.

*A classroom research-based term developed for *Math Expressions*

dot array
An arrangement of dots in rows and columns.

E

elapsed time
The time that passes between the beginning and the end of an activity.

endpoint
The point at either end of a line segment or the beginning point of a ray.

endpoint   endpoint   endpoint

equation
A statement that two expressions are equal. It has an equal sign.

Examples:
$32 + 35 = 67$
$67 = 32 + 34 + 1$
$(7 \times 8) + 1 = 57$

equilateral triangle
Having all sides of equal length.

equivalent fractions
Two or more fractions that represent the same number.

Example:
$\frac{2}{4}$ and $\frac{4}{8}$ are equivalent because they both represent one half.

estimate
A number close to an exact amount or to find about how many or how much.

evaluate an expression
Substitute a value for a letter (or symbol) and then simplify the expression.

expanded form
A way of writing a number that shows the value of each of its digits.

Example:
Expanded form of 835:
$800 + 30 + 5$
8 hundreds + 3 tens + 5 ones

Expanded Notation Method*
A method used to solve multiplication and division problems.

Examples:

$$\boxed{43 \times 67}$$

$$
\begin{array}{r}
67 = 60 + 7 \\
\times\, 43 = 40 + 3 \\
\hline
40 \times 60 = 2400 \\
40 \times 7 \ = \ 280 \\
3 \times 60 \ = \ 180 \\
3 \times 7 \ = \ +\ 21 \\
\hline
2{,}881
\end{array}
$$

$$\boxed{3{,}822 \div 7}$$

$$
\begin{array}{r}
6 \\
40\ \overline{)\,546} \\
500 \\
7\,\overline{)\,3{,}822} \\
-\ 3\ 500 \\
\hline
322 \\
-\ 280 \\
\hline
42 \\
-\ 42 \\
\hline
0
\end{array}
$$

*A classroom research-based term developed for *Math Expressions*

Glossary

expression

A number, variable, or a combination of numbers and variables with one or more operations.

Examples:

4

$6x$

$6x - 5$

$7 + 4$

F

factor

One of two or more numbers multiplied to find a product.

Example:

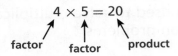

$4 \times 5 = 20$

factor   factor   product

factor pair

A factor pair for a number is a pair of whole numbers whose product is that number.

Example:

$5 \times 7 = 35$

factor   product
pair

fluid ounce (fl oz)

A unit of liquid volume in the customary system.

8 fluid ounces = 1 cup

foot (ft)

A U.S. customary unit of length equal to 12 inches.

---

formula

An equation with letters or symbols that describes a rule.

The formula for the area of a rectangle is:

$A = l \times w$

where A is the area, l is the length, and w is the width.

fraction

A number that is the sum of unit fractions, each an equal part of a set or part of a whole.

Examples:

$\frac{3}{4} = \frac{1}{4} + \frac{1}{4} + \frac{1}{4}$

$\frac{5}{4} = \frac{1}{4} + \frac{1}{4} + \frac{1}{4} + \frac{1}{4} + \frac{1}{4}$

G

gallon (gal)

A unit of liquid volume in the customary system that equals 4 quarts.

gram (g)

The basic unit of mass in the metric system.

greater than (>)

A symbol used to compare two numbers. The greater number is given first below.

Example:

33 > 17

33 is greater than 17.

group

To combine numbers to form new tens, hundreds, thousands, and so on.

H

hundredth

A unit fraction representing one of one hundred parts, written as 0.01 or $\frac{1}{100}$.

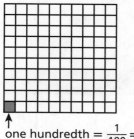

7.634
↑
hundredth

one hundredth = $\frac{1}{100}$ = 0.01

I

Identity Property of Multiplication

The product of 1 and any number equals that number.

Example:
$10 \times 1 = 10$

inch

A U.S. customary unit of length.

Example:

|← 1 inch →|

inequality

A statement that two expressions are not equal.

Examples:
$2 < 5$
$4 + 5 > 12 - 8$

inverse operations

Opposite or reverse operations that undo each other. Addition and subtraction are inverse operations. Multiplication and division are inverse operations.

Examples:
$4 + 6 = 10$ so, $10 - 6 = 4$ and $10 - 4 = 6$.
$3 \times 9 = 27$ so, $27 \div 9 = 3$ and $27 \div 3 = 9$.

isosceles triangle

A triangle with at least two sides of equal length.

K

kilogram (kg)

A unit of mass in the metric system that equals one thousand grams.

1 kg = 1,000 g

kiloliter (kL)

A unit of liquid volume in the metric system that equals one thousand liters.

1 kL = 1,000 L

kilometer (km)

A unit of length in the metric system that equals 1,000 meters.

1 km = 1,000 m

L

least common denominator

The least common multiple of two or more denominators.

Example:
The least common denominator of $\frac{1}{2}$ and $\frac{1}{3}$ is 6 because 6 is the smallest multiple of 2 and 3.

length

The measure of a line segment or the distance across the longer side of a rectangle

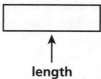

length

Glossary

less than (<)
A symbol used to compare two numbers. The smaller number is given first below.

Example:
54 < 78
54 is less than 78.

line
A straight path that goes on forever in opposite directions.

Example:
line *AB*

line of symmetry
A line on which a figure can be folded so that the two halves match exactly.

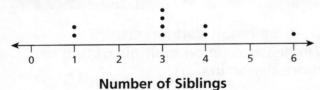

line plot
A diagram that shows the frequency of data on a number line. Also called a dot plot.

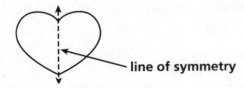

Number of Siblings

line segment
Part of a line that has two endpoints.

line symmetry
A figure has line symmetry if it can be folded along a line to create two halves that match exactly.

liquid volume
A measure of the space a liquid occupies.

liter (L)
The basic unit of liquid volume in the metric system.
1 liter = 1,000 milliliters

M

mass
The measure of the amount of matter in an object.

meter (m)
The basic unit of length in the metric system.

metric system
A base ten system of measurement.

mile (mi)
A U.S. customary unit of length equal to 5,280 feet.

milligram (mg)
A unit of mass in the metric system.
1,000 mg = 1g

milliliter (mL)
A unit of liquid volume in the metric system. 1,000 mL = 1 L

millimeter (mm)
A unit of length in the metric system.
1,000 mm = 1 m

mixed number
A number that can be represented by a whole number and a fraction.

Example:
$4\frac{1}{2} = 4 + \frac{1}{2}$

multiple
A number that is the product of a given number and any whole number.

Examples:
$4 \times 1 = 4$, so 4 is a multiple of 4.
$4 \times 2 = 8$, so 8 is a multiple of 4.

N

number line
A line that extends, without end, in each direction and shows numbers as a series of points. The location of each number is shown by its distance from 0.

numerator
The number above the bar in a fraction. It shows the number of equal parts.

Example:

$\frac{3}{4} \longleftarrow$ numerator $\frac{3}{4} = \frac{1}{4} + \frac{1}{4} + \frac{1}{4}$

O

obtuse angle
An angle greater than a right angle and less than a straight angle.

obtuse triangle
A triangle with one obtuse angle.

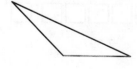

opposite sides
Sides that are across from each other; they do not meet at a point.

Example:
Sides a and c are opposite.

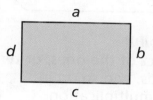

Order of Operations
A set of rules that state the order in which operations should be done.

STEP 1: Compute inside parentheses first.

STEP 2: Multiply and divide from left to right.

STEP 3: Add and subtract from left to right.

ounce (oz)
A unit of weight.

16 ounces = 1 pound

A unit of liquid volume (also called a fluid ounce).

8 ounces = 1 cup

P

parallel lines
Lines in the same plane that never intersect are parallel. Line segments and rays that are part of parallel lines are also parallel.

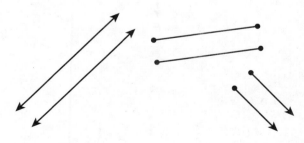

parallelogram

A quadrilateral with both pairs of opposite sides parallel.

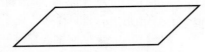

partial product

The product of the ones, or tens, or hundreds, and so on in multidigit multiplication.

Example:

```
    24
  ×  9
  ────
    36   ←  partial product (9 × 4)
   180   ←  partial product (9 × 20)
  ────
   216
```

pattern

A sequence that can be described by a rule.

perimeter

The distance around a figure.

perpendicular lines

Lines, line segments, or rays are perpendicular if they form right angles.

Example:

These two lines are perpendicular.

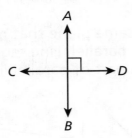

pictograph

A graph that uses pictures or symbols to represent data.

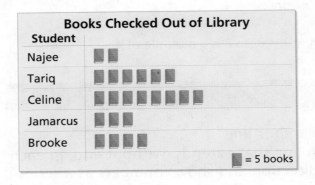

pint (pt)

A customary unit of liquid volume that equals 16 fluid ounces.

place value

The value assigned to the place that a digit occupies in a number.

Example:

235

The 2 is in the hundreds place, so its value is 200.

place value drawing*

A drawing that represents a number. Thousands are represented by vertical rectangles, hundreds are represented by squares, tens are represented by vertical lines, and ones by small circles.

Example:

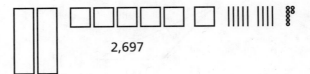

2,697

*A classroom research-based term developed for *Math Expressions*

Place Value Sections Method*
A method using rectangle drawings to solve multiplication or division problems.

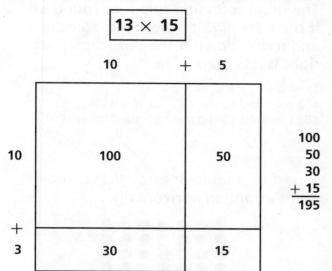

point
A location in a plane. It is usually shown by a dot.

polygon
A closed plane figure with sides made of straight line segments.

pound (lb)
A unit of weight in the U.S. customary system.

prefix
A letter or group of letters placed before a word to make a new word.

prime number
A number greater than 1 that has 1 and itself as the only factor pair. Examples of prime numbers are 2, 7, and 13. The only factor pair of 7 is 1 and 7.

product
The answer to a multiplication problem.

Example:

$9 \times 7 = 63$

product

protractor
A semicircular tool for measuring and constructing angles.

Q

quadrilateral
A polygon with four sides.

quart (qt)
A customary unit of liquid volume that equals 32 ounces or 4 cups.

quotient
The answer to a division problem.

Example:

$$9\overline{)63}$$

7 is the quotient.

R

ray
Part of a line that has one endpoint and extends without end in one direction.

*A classroom research-based term developed for *Math Expressions*

Glossary

rectangle

A parallelogram with four right angles.

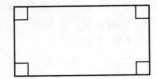

reflex angle

An angle with a measure that is greater than 180° and less than 360°.

remainder

The number left over after dividing two numbers that are not evenly divisible.

Example:

$$5\overline{)43}\ \ \ ^{8\ R3}$$ The remainder is 3.

rhombus

A parallelogram with sides of equal length.

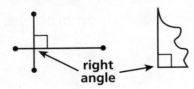

right angle

One of four angles made by perpendicular line segments.

right
angle

right triangle

A triangle with one right angle.

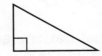

rounding

Finding the nearest ten, hundred, thousand, or some other place value. The usual rounding rule is to round up if the next digit to the right is 5 or more and round down if the next digit to the right is less than 5.

Examples:

463 rounded to the nearest ten is 460.
463 rounded to the nearest hundred is 500.

row

A part of a table or array that contains items arranged horizontally.

S

scalene triangle

A triangle with no equal sides is a scalene triangle.

Shortcut Method*

A strategy for multiplying. It is the current common method in the United States.

Step 1	Step 2
^{7} 28	^{7} 28
× 9	× 9
2	252

*A classroom research-based term developed for *Math Expressions*

simplest form

A fraction is in simplest form if there is no whole number (other than 1) that divides evenly into the numerator and denominator.

Example:

$\frac{3}{4}$ This fraction is in simplest form because no number divides evenly into 3 and 4.

simplify an expression

Combining like terms and performing operations until all possible terms have been combined.

simplify a fraction

Dividing the numerator and the denominator of a fraction by the same number to make an equivalent fraction made from fewer but larger unit fractions.

Example:

$\frac{5}{10} = \frac{5 \div 5}{10 \div 5} = \frac{1}{2}$

situation equation*

An equation that shows the structure of the information in a problem.

Example:

$35 + n = 40$

solution equation*

An equation that shows the operation that can be used to solve the problem.

Example:

$n = 40 - 35$

square

A rectangle with 4 sides of equal length and 4 right angles. It is also a rhombus.

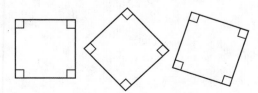

square array

An array in which the number of rows equals the number of columns.

square centimeter (cm²)

A unit of area equal to the area of a square with one-centimeter sides.

square decimeter (dm²)

A unit of area equal to the area of a square with one-decimeter sides.

square foot (ft²)

A unit of area equal to the area of a square with one-foot sides.

square inch (in.²)

A unit of area equal to the area of a square with one-inch sides.

square kilometer (km²)

A unit of area equal to the area of a square with one-kilometer sides.

square meter (m²)

A unit of area equal to the area of a square with one-meter sides.

square mile (mi²)

A unit of area equal to the area of a square with one-mile sides.

square millimeter (mm²)

A unit of area equal to the area of a square with one-millimeter sides.

*A classroom research-based term developed for *Math Expressions*

Glossary

square unit (unit²)
A unit of area equal to the area of a square with one-unit sides.

square yard (yd²)
A unit of area equal to the area of a square with one-yard sides.

standard form
The form of a number written using digits.

Example:
2,145

straight angle
An angle that measures 180°.

sum
The answer when adding two or more addends.

Example:

$$53 + 26 = 79$$

addend   addend   sum

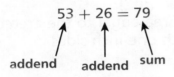

T

table
Data arranged in rows and columns.

tenth
A unit fraction representing one of ten equal parts of a whole, written as 0.1 or $\frac{1}{10}$.

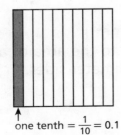

12.34
↑
tenth

one tenth = $\frac{1}{10}$ = 0.1

term
A number, variable, product, or quotient in an expression or equation. Each term is separated by an operation sign (+, −).

Example:
$3n + 5$ has two terms, $3n$ and 5.

thousandth
A unit fraction representing one of one thousand equal parts of a whole, written as 0.001 or $\frac{1}{1,000}$.

ton
A unit of weight that equals 2,000 pounds.

tonne
A metric unit of mass that equals 1,000 kilograms.

total
Sum. The result of addition.

Example:

$$53 + 26 = 79$$

addend   addend   total (sum)

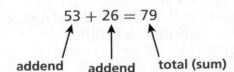

trapezoid
A quadrilateral with exactly one pair of parallel sides.

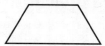

triangle
A polygon with three sides.

U

unit
A standard of measurement.

Examples:
Centimeters, pounds, inches, and so on.

unit fraction
A fraction whose numerator is 1. It shows one equal part of a whole.

Example:

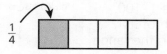

$\frac{1}{4}$

V

variable
A letter or a symbol that represents a number in an algebraic expression.

vertex of an angle
A point that is shared by two sides of an angle.

vertex

vertex of a polygon
A point that is shared by two sides of a polygon.

vertex

W

width
The distance across the shorter side of a rectangle.

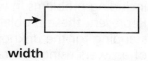

width

word form
The form of a number written using words instead of digits.

Example:
Six hundred thirty-nine

Y

yard (yd)
A U.S. customary unit of length equal to 3 feet.

4.OA Operations and Algebraic Thinking

Use the four operations with whole numbers to solve problems.

4.OA.A.1	Interpret a multiplication equation as a comparison, e.g., interpret $35 = 5 \times 7$ as a statement that 35 is 5 times as many as 7 and 7 times as many as 5. Represent verbal statements of multiplicative comparisons as multiplication equations.	Unit 4 Lessons 4, 5, 6, 12
4.OA.A.2	Multiply or divide to solve word problems involving multiplicative comparison, e.g., by using drawings and equations with a symbol for the unknown number to represent the problem, distinguishing multiplicative comparison from additive comparison.	Unit 4 Lessons 4, 5, 6, 12
4.OA.A.3	Solve multistep word problems posed with whole numbers and having whole-number answers using the four operations, including problems in which remainders must be interpreted. Represent these problems using equations with a letter standing for the unknown quantity. Assess the reasonableness of answers using mental computation and estimation strategies including rounding.	Unit 1 Lessons 8, 11, 12 Unit 2 Lessons 11, 15, 17, 18, 19 Unit 3 Lessons 8, 9, 10, 11 Unit 4 Lessons 7, 8, 9, 12

Gain familiarity with factors and multiples.

4.OA.B.4	Find all factor pairs for a whole number in the range 1–100. Recognize that a whole number is a multiple of each of its factors. Determine whether a given whole number in the range 1–100 is a multiple of a given one-digit number. Determine whether a given whole number in the range 1–100 is prime or composite.	Unit 4 Lessons 10, 12

Generate and analyze patterns.

4.OA.C.5	Generate a number or shape pattern that follows a given rule. Identify apparent features of the pattern that were not explicit in the rule itself.	Unit 4 Lessons 10, 11, 12 Unit 8 Lesson 12

■ **Major**　　■ **Supporting**　　■ **Additional**

4.NBT Number and Operations in Base Ten

Generalize place value understanding for multi-digit whole numbers.

4.NBT.A.1	Recognize that in a multi-digit whole number, a digit in one place represents ten times what it represents in the place to its right.	Unit 1 Lessons 1, 2, 4 Unit 2 Lessons 2, 3
4.NBT.A.2	Read and write multi-digit whole numbers using base-ten numerals, number names, and expanded form. Compare two multi-digit numbers based on meanings of the digits in each place, using >, =, and < symbols to record the results of comparisons.	Unit 1 Lessons 2, 3, 4, 5 Unit 2 Lessons 4, 10, 12, 16, 19
4.NBT.A.3	Use place value understanding to round multi-digit whole numbers to any place.	Unit 1 Lessons 3, 5, 8, 11, 14 Unit 2 Lessons 5, 17 Unit 3 Lesson 8

Use place value understanding and properties of operations to perform multi-digit arithmetic.

4.NBT.B.4	Fluently add and subtract multi-digit whole numbers using the standard algorithm.	Unit 1 Lessons 6, 7, 8, 9, 10, 11, 12, 13, 14 Unit 4 Lessons 1, 2, 12
4.NBT.B.5	Multiply a whole number of up to four digits by a one-digit whole number, and multiply two two-digit numbers, using strategies based on place value and the properties of operations. Illustrate and explain the calculation by using equations, rectangular arrays, and/or area models.	Unit 2 Lessons 1, 2, 3, 4, 5, 6, 7, 8, 9, 10, 11, 12, 13, 14, 15, 16, 17, 18, 19 Unit 4 Lessons 1, 3, 12
4.NBT.B.6	Find whole-number quotients and remainders with up to four-digit dividends and one-digit divisors, using strategies based on place value, the properties of operations, and/or the relationship between multiplication and division. Illustrate and explain the calculation by using equations, rectangular arrays, and/or area models.	Unit 3 Lessons 1, 2, 3, 4, 5, 6, 7, 8, 9, 10, 11 Unit 4 Lessons 1, 3, 4, 12

Common Core State Standards for Mathematical Content

4.NF Number and Operations—Fractions

Extend understanding of fraction equivalence and ordering.

4.NF.A.1	Explain why a fraction $\frac{a}{b}$ is equivalent to a fraction $\frac{(n \times a)}{(n \times b)}$ by using visual fraction models, with attention to how the number and size of the parts differ even though the two fractions themselves are the same size. Use this principle to recognize and generate equivalent fractions.	Unit 7 Lessons 4, 5, 6, 13
4.NF.A.2	Compare two fractions with different numerators and different denominators, e.g., by creating common denominators or numerators, or by comparing to a benchmark fraction such as $\frac{1}{2}$. Recognize that comparisons are valid only when the two fractions refer to the same whole. Record the results of comparisons with symbols >, =, or <, and justify the conclusions, e.g., by using a visual fraction model.	Unit 6 Lessons 2, 4, 5, 10 Unit 7 Lessons 1, 2, 3, 6, 13

Build fractions from unit fractions by applying and extending previous understandings of operations on whole numbers.

4.NF.B.3	Understand a fraction $\frac{a}{b}$ with $a > 1$ as a sum of fractions $\frac{1}{b}$.	Unit 6 Lessons 1, 2, 3, 4, 5, 6
4.NF.B.3.a	Understand addition and subtraction of fractions as joining and separating parts referring to the same whole.	Unit 6 Lessons 2, 3, 4, 5, 6, 10
4.NF.B.3.b	Decompose a fraction into a sum of fractions with the same denominator in more than one way, recording each decomposition by an equation. Justify decompositions, e.g., by using a visual fraction model.	Unit 6 Lessons 2, 4, 6
4.NF.B.3.c	Add and subtract mixed numbers with like denominators, e.g., by replacing each mixed number with an equivalent fraction, and/or by using properties of operations and the relationship between addition and subtraction.	Unit 6 Lessons 5, 6, 9, 10
4.NF.B.3.d	Solve word problems involving addition and subtraction of fractions referring to the same whole and having like denominators, e.g., by using visual fraction models and equations to represent the problem.	Unit 6 Lessons 3, 4, 6, 9, 10
4.NF.B.4	Apply and extend previous understandings of multiplication to multiply a fraction by a whole number.	Unit 6 Lessons 7, 8, 9
4.NF.B.4.a	Understand a fraction $\frac{a}{b}$ as a multiple of $\frac{1}{b}$.	Unit 6 Lessons 1, 7, 8, 9
4.NF.B.4.b	Understand a multiple of $\frac{a}{b}$ as a multiple of $\frac{1}{b}$, and use this understanding to multiply a fraction by a whole number.	Unit 6 Lessons 7, 8, 9
4.NF.B.4.c	Solve word problems involving multiplication of a fraction by a whole number, e.g., by using visual fraction models and equations to represent the problem.	Unit 6 Lessons 7, 8, 9, 10

■ **Major**　■ **Supporting**　■ **Additional**

Understand decimal notation for fractions, and compare decimal fractions.

4.NF.C.5	Express a fraction with denominator 10 as an equivalent fraction with denominator 100, and use this technique to add two fractions with respective denominators 10 and 100.	Unit 7 Lesson 6
4.NF.C.6	Use decimal notation for fractions with denominators 10 or 100.	Unit 7 Lessons 8, 9, 10, 11, 13
4.NF.C.7	Compare two decimals to hundredths by reasoning about their size. Recognize that comparisons are valid only when the two decimals refer to the same whole. Record the results of comparisons with the symbols >, =, or <, and justify the conclusions, e.g., by using a visual model.	Unit 7 Lessons 10, 12, 13

4.MD Measurement and Data

Solve problems involving measurement and conversion of measurements from a larger unit to a smaller unit.

4.MD.A.1	Know relative sizes of measurement units within one system of units including km, m, cm; kg, g; lb, oz.; l, ml; hr, min, sec. Within a single system of measurement, express measurements in a larger unit in terms of a smaller unit. Record measurement equivalents in a two-column table.	Unit 5 Lessons 1, 2, 3, 4, 5, 7, 8
4.MD.A.2	Use the four operations to solve word problems involving distances, intervals of time, liquid volumes, masses of objects, and money, including problems involving simple fractions or decimals, and problems that require expressing measurements given in a larger unit in terms of a smaller unit. Represent measurement quantities using diagrams such as number line diagrams that feature a measurement scale.	Unit 1 Lessons 6, 13, 14 Unit 2 Lessons 4, 6, 10, 11, 18, 19 Unit 3 Lesson 8 Unit 4 Lessons 7, 8, 12 Unit 5 Lessons 1, 2, 3, 4, 5, 7, 8 Unit 6 Lessons 3, 6, 7, 8, 9, 10 Unit 7 Lessons 10, 12
4.MD.A.3	Apply the area and perimeter formulas for rectangles in real world and mathematical problems.	Unit 5 Lessons 6, 7, 8

Represent and interpret data.

4.MD.B.4	Make a line plot to display a data set of measurements in fractions of a unit ($\frac{1}{2}$, $\frac{1}{4}$, $\frac{1}{8}$). Solve problems involving addition and subtraction of fractions by using information presented in line plots.	Unit 5 Lesson 3 Unit 6 Lesson 6 Unit 7 Lessons 7, 13

Common Core State Standards for Mathematical Content

Geometric measurement: understand concepts of angle and measure angles.

4.MD.C.5	Recognize angles as geometric shapes that are formed wherever two rays share a common endpoint, and understand concepts of angle measurement:	Unit 8 Lessons 1, 2, 3
4.MD.C.5.a	An angle is measured with reference to a circle with its center at the common endpoint of the rays, by considering the fraction of the circular arc between the points where the two rays intersect the circle. An angle that turns through $\frac{1}{360}$ of a circle is called a "one-degree angle," and can be used to measure angles.	Unit 8 Lessons 2, 3
4.MD.C.5.b	An angle that turns through n one-degree angles is said to have an angle measure of n degrees.	Unit 8 Lessons 2, 3
4.MD.C.6	Measure angles in whole-number degrees using a protractor. Sketch angles of specified measure.	Unit 8 Lessons 2, 3, 5
4.MD.C.7	Recognize angle measure as additive. When an angle is decomposed into non-overlapping parts, the angle measure of the whole is the sum of the angle measures of the parts. Solve addition and subtraction problems to find unknown angles on a diagram in real world and mathematical problems, e.g., by using an equation with a symbol for the unknown angle measure.	Unit 8 Lessons 3, 5, 6

4.G Geometry

Draw and identify lines and angles, and classify shapes by properties of their lines and angles.

4.G.A.1	Draw points, lines, line segments, rays, angles (right, acute, obtuse), and perpendicular and parallel lines. Identify these in two-dimensional figures.	Unit 8 Lessons 1, 2, 3, 4, 5, 7, 8, 9, 10, 12
4.G.A.2	Classify two-dimensional figures based on the presence or absence of parallel or perpendicular lines, or the presence or absence of angles of a specified size. Recognize right triangles as a category, and identify right triangles.	Unit 8 Lessons 4, 8, 9, 10, 12
4.G.A.3	Recognize a line of symmetry for a two-dimensional figure as a line across the figure such that the figure can be folded along the line into matching parts. Identify line-symmetric figures and draw lines of symmetry.	Unit 8 Lessons 11, 12

■ **Major**   ■ **Supporting**   ■ **Additional**

MP1 Make sense of problems and persevere in solving them.

Mathematically proficient students start by explaining to themselves the meaning of a problem and looking for entry points to its solution. They analyze givens, constraints, relationships, and goals. They make conjectures about the form and meaning of the solution and plan a solution pathway rather than simply jumping into a solution attempt. They consider analogous problems, and try special cases and simpler forms of the original problem in order to gain insight into its solution. They monitor and evaluate their progress and change course if necessary. Older students might, depending on the context of the problem, transform algebraic expressions or change the viewing window on their graphing calculator to get the information they need. Mathematically proficient students can explain correspondences between equations, verbal descriptions, tables, and graphs or draw diagrams of important features and relationships, graph data, and search for regularity or trends. Younger students might rely on using concrete objects or pictures to help conceptualize and solve a problem. Mathematically proficient students check their answers to problems using a different method, and they continually ask themselves, "Does this make sense?" They can understand the approaches of others to solving complex problems and identify correspondences between different approaches.

Unit 1 Lessons 2, 5, 6, 7, 8, 10, 11, 12, 13, 14
Unit 2 Lessons 2, 3, 4, 5, 6, 7, 10, 11, 13, 14, 15, 16, 17, 18, 19
Unit 3 Lessons 2, 5, 6, 7, 8, 9, 10, 11
Unit 4 Lessons 2, 3, 4, 5, 6, 7, 8, 9, 12
Unit 5 Lessons 1, 2, 3, 4, 5, 6, 7, 8
Unit 6 Lessons 5, 6, 7, 10
Unit 7 Lessons 1, 2, 3, 4, 5, 6, 7, 8, 9, 10, 11, 13
Unit 8 Lessons 5, 6, 7, 8, 12

MP2 Reason abstractly and quantitatively.

Mathematically proficient students make sense of quantities and their relationships in problem situations. They bring two complementary abilities to bear on problems involving quantitative relationships: the ability to *decontextualize*—to abstract a given situation and represent it symbolically and manipulate the representing symbols as if they have a life of their own, without necessarily attending to their referents—and the ability to *contextualize*, to pause as needed during the manipulation process in order to probe into the referents for the symbols involved. Quantitative reasoning entails habits of creating a coherent representation of the problem at hand; considering the units involved; attending to the meaning of quantities, not just how to compute them; and knowing and flexibly using different properties of operations and objects.

Unit 1 Lessons 1, 3, 4, 5, 6, 8, 9, 14
Unit 2 Lessons 2, 4, 5, 6, 7, 8, 9, 10, 11, 13, 15, 16, 17, 19
Unit 3 Lessons 1, 3, 5, 7, 8, 11
Unit 4 Lessons 1, 2, 3, 4, 5, 6, 12
Unit 5 Lessons 2, 6, 7, 8
Unit 6 Lessons 1, 2, 3, 4, 7, 10
Unit 7 Lessons 1, 2, 9, 10, 13
Unit 8 Lessons 3, 5, 6, 12

MP3 Construct viable arguments and critique the reasoning of others.

Mathematically proficient students understand and use stated assumptions, definitions, and previously established results in constructing arguments. They make conjectures and build a logical progression of statements to explore the truth of their conjectures. They are able to analyze situations by breaking them into cases, and can recognize and use counterexamples. They justify their conclusions, communicate them to others, and respond to the arguments of others. They reason inductively about data, making plausible arguments that take into account the context from which the data arose. Mathematically proficient students are also able to compare the effectiveness of two plausible arguments, distinguish correct logic or reasoning from that which is flawed, and—if there is a flaw in an argument—explain what it is. Elementary students can construct arguments using concrete referents such as objects, drawings, diagrams, and actions. Such arguments can make sense and be correct, even though they are not generalized or made formal until later grades. Later, students learn to determine domains to which an argument applies. Students at all grades can listen or read the arguments of others, decide whether they make sense, and ask useful questions to clarify or improve the arguments.

Unit 1 Lessons 1, 2, 3, 4, 5, 6, 7, 8, 9, 10, 11, 12, 13, 14
Unit 2 Lessons 1, 2, 3, 4, 5, 6, 7, 8, 9, 10, 11, 12, 13, 14, 15, 16, 17, 18, 19
Unit 3 Lessons 1, 2, 3, 4, 5, 6, 7, 8, 9, 10, 11
Unit 4 Lessons 1, 2, 3, 4, 5, 6, 7, 8, 9, 10, 11, 12
Unit 5 Lessons 1, 2, 3, 4, 5, 6, 7, 8
Unit 6 Lessons 1, 2, 3, 4, 5, 6, 7, 8, 9, 10
Unit 7 Lessons 1, 2, 3, 4, 5, 6, 7, 8, 9, 10, 11, 12, 13
Unit 8 Lessons 1, 2, 3, 4, 5, 6, 7, 8, 9, 10, 11, 12

MP4 Model with mathematics.

Mathematically proficient students can apply the mathematics they know to solve problems arising in everyday life, society, and the workplace. In early grades, this might be as simple as writing an addition equation to describe a situation. In middle grades, a student might apply proportional reasoning to plan a school event or analyze a problem in the community. By high school, a student might use geometry to solve a design problem or use a function to describe how one quantity of interest depends on another. Mathematically proficient students who can apply what they know are comfortable making assumptions and approximations to simplify a complicated situation, realizing that these may need revision later. They are able to identify important quantities in a practical situation and map their relationships using such tools as diagrams, two-way tables, graphs, flowcharts and formulas. They can analyze those relationships mathematically to draw conclusions. They routinely interpret their mathematical results in the context of the situation and reflect on whether the results make sense, possibly improving the model if it has not served its purpose.

Unit 1 Lessons 1, 2, 3, 4, 6, 9, 10, 12, 13, 14
Unit 2 Lessons 1, 2, 4, 5, 6, 7, 8, 12, 16, 19
Unit 3 Lessons 1, 3, 4, 10, 11
Unit 4 Lessons 2, 3, 4, 5, 8, 9, 10, 12
Unit 5 Lessons 4, 7, 8
Unit 6 Lessons 1, 3, 4, 5, 6, 7, 8, 10
Unit 7 Lessons 2, 3, 5, 7, 8, 10, 13
Unit 8 Lessons 6, 12

MP5 Use appropriate tools strategically.

Mathematically proficient students consider the available tools when solving a mathematical problem. These tools might include pencil and paper, concrete models, a ruler, a protractor, a calculator, a spreadsheet, a computer algebra system, a statistical package, or dynamic geometry software. Proficient students are sufficiently familiar with tools appropriate for their grade or course to make sound decisions about when each of these tools might be helpful, recognizing both the insight to be gained and their limitations. For example, mathematically proficient high school students analyze graphs of functions and solutions generated using a graphing calculator. They detect possible errors by strategically using estimation and other mathematical knowledge. When making mathematical models, they know that technology can enable them to visualize the results of varying assumptions, explore consequences, and compare predictions with data. Mathematically proficient students at various grade levels are able to identify relevant external mathematical resources, such as digital content located on a website, and use them to pose or solve problems. They are able to use technological tools to explore and deepen their understanding of concepts.

Unit 1 Lessons 1, 2, 3, 4, 6, 9, 14
Unit 2 Lessons 1, 4, 5, 6, 7, 8, 10, 11, 12, 16, 19
Unit 3 Lessons 3, 4, 11
Unit 4 Lessons 2, 10, 12
Unit 5 Lessons 1, 4, 5, 6, 7, 8
Unit 6 Lessons 1, 2, 3, 4, 8, 9, 10
Unit 7 Lessons 1, 2, 4, 5, 9, 10, 11, 12, 13
Unit 8 Lessons 1, 2, 4, 5, 7, 8, 9, 10, 11, 12

MP6 Attend to precision.

Mathematically proficient students try to communicate precisely to others. They try to use clear definitions in discussion with others and in their own reasoning. They state the meaning of the symbols they choose, including using the equal sign consistently and appropriately. They are careful about specifying units of measure, and labeling axes to clarify the correspondence with quantities in a problem. They calculate accurately and efficiently, expressing numerical answers with a degree of precision appropriate for the problem context. In the elementary grades, students give carefully formulated explanations to each other. By the time they reach high school they have learned to examine claims and make explicit use of definitions.

Unit 1 Lessons 1, 2, 3, 4, 5, 6, 7, 8, 9, 10, 11, 12, 13, 14
Unit 2 Lessons 1, 2, 3, 4, 5, 6, 7, 8, 9, 10, 11, 12, 13, 14, 15, 16, 17, 18, 19
Unit 3 Lessons 1, 2, 3, 4, 5, 6, 7, 8, 9, 10, 11
Unit 4 Lessons 1, 2, 3, 4, 5, 6, 7, 8, 9, 10, 11, 12
Unit 5 Lessons 1, 2, 3, 4, 5, 6, 7, 8
Unit 6 Lessons 1, 2, 3, 4, 5, 6, 7, 8, 9, 10
Unit 7 Lessons 1, 2, 3, 4, 5, 6, 7, 8, 9, 10, 11, 12, 13
Unit 8 Lessons 1, 2, 3, 4, 5, 6, 7, 8, 9, 10, 11, 12

Common Core State Standards for Mathematical Practice

MP7 Look for and make use of structure.

Mathematically proficient students look closely to discern a pattern or structure. Young students, for example, might notice that three and seven more is the same amount as seven and three more, or they may sort a collection of shapes according to how many sides the shapes have. Later, students will see 7×8 equals the well-remembered $7 \times 5 + 7 \times 3$, in preparation for learning about the distributive property. In the expression $x^2 + 9x + 14$, older students can see the 14 as 2×7 and the 9 as $2 + 7$. They recognize the significance of an existing line in a geometric figure and can use the strategy of drawing an auxiliary line for solving problems. They also can step back for an overview and shift perspective. They can see complicated things, such as some algebraic expressions, as single objects or as being composed of several objects. For example, they can see $5 - 3(x - y)^2$ as 5 minus a positive number times a square and use that to realize that its value cannot be more than 5 for any real numbers x and y.

Unit 1 Lessons 1, 2, 4, 9, 13, 14
Unit 2 Lessons 2, 3, 6, 8, 9, 10, 13, 16, 17, 19
Unit 3 Lessons 1, 3, 10, 11
Unit 4 Lessons 1, 2, 3, 5, 10, 11, 12
Unit 5 Lessons 1, 2, 4, 8
Unit 6 Lessons 1, 4, 5, 10
Unit 7 Lessons 2, 6, 9, 10, 11, 12, 13
Unit 8 Lessons 1, 2, 4, 7, 8, 9, 10

MP8 Look for and express regularity in repeated reasoning.

Mathematically proficient students notice if calculations are repeated, and look both for general methods and for shortcuts. Upper elementary students might notice when dividing 25 by 11 that they are repeating the same calculations over and over again, and conclude they have a repeating decimal. By paying attention to the calculation of slope as they repeatedly check whether points are on the line through (1, 2) with slope 3, middle school students might abstract the equation $(y - 2)/(x - 1) = 3$. Noticing the regularity in the way terms cancel when expanding $(x - 1)(x + 1)$, $(x - 1)(x^2 + x + 1)$, and $(x - 1)(x^3 + x^2 + x + 1)$ might lead them to the general formula for the sum of a geometric series. As they work to solve a problem, mathematically proficient students maintain oversight of the process, while attending to the details. They continually evaluate the reasonableness of their intermediate results.

Unit 1 Lessons 3, 4, 5, 6, 7, 10, 11, 14
Unit 2 Lessons 1, 2, 3, 5, 7, 8, 15, 17, 19
Unit 3 Lessons 1, 3, 5, 6, 11
Unit 4 Lessons 1, 2, 10, 11, 12
Unit 5 Lessons 1, 4, 6, 8
Unit 6 Lessons 2, 7, 9, 10
Unit 7 Lessons 1, 3, 6, 8, 10, 11, 13
Unit 8 Lessons 1, 3, 4, 9, 10, 11, 12

A

Acute angle, 359–360, 395

Acute triangle, 363–364, 367–368, 387–390

Addend, 29, 36–37, 164, 165, 256, 259, 269, 330

Adding up to subtract, 33

Addition
align places, 20, 22
angle measures, 369–370
break-apart drawings, 29
chains, 309, 312–314
comparisons, 173–176, 177
fractions, 249–262, 267, 269–271, 281–282, 318, 326
grouping, 17–18
mental math, 21–22
methods, 17, 19
  New Groups Above, 17–19
  New Groups Below, 17–19
  Show Subtotals, 17–19
with money, 18
multidigit, 17–22, 29–30, 31, 34–36, 145–146
patterns, 195
related to,
  multiplication, 275–276, 279, 281
  place value, 8, 12, 17, 19–20, 22
  subtraction, 29–30, 31, 164
with units of time, 222

Additive comparison, 173–176, 177–178

Algebra
equations. *See* Equations, numerical; Inequality.
expressions
  evaluate expressions
    using order of operations, 161, 162
    using properties, 161
inequalities, 10, 13, 257, 297, 315–318, 331, 336
inverse relationships. *See* Inverse Operations.
situation equations, 163–164, 165–168

solution equations, 163–164, 165–166
solving equations,
  addition and subtraction, 163–164, 165–166, 177–178
  multiplication and division, 71,173–174, 175–176, 177–178
  multi-step, 183–188
  one-step, 165–166, 168, 171–172, 173–176, 177–178
  two-step, 181–182
using a variable to represent an unknown, 165–166, 168, 171–172, 173–176, 177–178
writing equations, 33, 36–37, 132, 145–146, 163–166, 167–168, 171–172, 173–176, 177–178, 181–182, 183–185, 187–188, 197–198, 262, 271, 277–278, 280, 282, 283–284, 369, 371, 373–374

Adjacent sides, 383

Algebraic language, 70, 76, 161–162

Angle Cut-Outs, 354A

Angles. *See also* Geometry, angle.
angle equations, 370–374, 373–374
classifying, 354–354A, 358, 359, 369–370, 395
compose, 369–370, 373
decompose, 371–372, 374
draw and describe, 352–354, 356–357, 360, 363, 369, 370–371
measuring, 355–360, 359–360, 369–372
naming, 352, 354, 365
reflex, 359
turns in a circle, 355, 359–360
types of
  acute, 354, 358, 359–360, 363–364, 367–368, 371, 387–388, 390, 395
  obtuse, 354, 358, 359–360, 363–364, 367–368, 371, 387–388, 390, 395
  right, 354, 355, 357–358, 359, 363–364, 367–368, 369, 371, 380–382, 387–388, 390–392, 395
  straight. 354, 355, 359–360, 369–372, 374
vertex of, 352

Index

Answers, reasonable, 38

Area, 53–54, 232–234, 236, 237–238
formulas, 232–233
of rectangles, 53–54, 61–62, 232–234, 236

Area models
division and, 117, 121–122, 125, 129, 133, 139
fractions and, 275
multiplication and, 53–54, 56, 61–62, 65, 67–68, 69–70, 71, 75–76, 85–86, 87, 95–96, 97

Arrays, 3–4, 53–54, 56
area and, 53, 233
columns, 53
dot, 3–4, 85–86
factor pairs and, 191–192
multiplication strategy, 53–54, 56, 85–86
rows, 53
units, 56

Assessment
On-Going Assessment
Fluency Check, 24, 42, 59, 60, 84, 94, 106, 138, 150, 170, 180, 190, 200, 230, 240, 264, 274, 286, 306, 322, 340, 362, 376, 394, 404
Quick Quiz, 15, 23, 41, 59, 83, 93, 105, 137, 149, 169, 179, 189, 199, 229, 239, 263, 273, 285, 305, 321, 339, 361, 375, 393, 403
Strategy Check, 16
Performance Assessment
Unit Performance Task, 49–50, 113–114, 157–158, 207–208, 247–248, 293–294, 347–348, 411–412
Summative Assessment
Unit Review/Test, 43–48, 107–112, 151–156, 201–206, 241–246, 287–292, 341–346, 405–410

Associative Property
of Addition, 22
of Multiplication, 54, 55–56, 95, 161

B

Bar graph
analyze, 39, 178
comparisons using, 178
horizontal, 39
make, 39
scale, 39
vertical, 178

C

Centimeter, 211–213, 231–232

Circle graph, 283

Circles. *See also* Graphs, circle.
angles and, 355, 359–360, 373

Common denominator, 316

Commutative Property
of Addition, 22, 161, 164
of Multiplication, 55–56, 77, 161

Compare, 171. *See also* Inequality.
decimals, 331, 335–336
fractions, 257–258, 268, 297–298, 300–304, 303–304, 315–318
whole numbers, 10, 13

Comparison
bars, 171–172, 173–176
language, 168, 173
problems, 171–172, 173–176, 177–178, 183–184, 277

Comparison problems, 171–172, 173–176, 177–178, 183–184, 198, 277

Composite number, 192, 194

Cup, 227–228

Customary measurement. *See* Measurement, customary.

D

Data Analysis
analyze data
from a bar graph, 39–40, 178
from a line plot, 220, 272, 284, 319–320

E

Index

F

Index

H

I

K

L

M

Index

Rectangle Model, 53–54, 56, 61–62, 65, 67–68, 69–70, 71, 75–76, 85–86, 87, 95–96, 97

Shortcut Method, 74, 88, 91, 97–98

money, 63–64, 78

multiples, 57–58, 65, 119, 193–194, 213–214, 215–218, 316

one-digit by four-digit, 95–96, 97–101

one-digit by three-digit, 75–78

patterns, 55, 57–58, 119, 194, 195

properties of

Associative Property, 55

Commutative Property, 55

Distributive Property, 69

relate to division, 117, 119, 121, 167

two-digit by one-digit, 54, 61–66, 65–66, 67–68, 69–70, 71–72, 73–74

two-digit by two-digit, 55–56, 85–86, 87–88, 89–90, 91–92

write equations, 61, 167–168, 171–172, 175–176, 277–278, 280–282

with zeros, 119

Multiplicative comparison, 171–172, 175–176

Multistep problems, 81–82, 146, 183–188

N

New Groups Above Method

1-Row Product, in multiplication, 74

in addition, 17, 19

New Groups Below Method

1-Row Product, in multiplication, 74, 88

in addition, 17, 19

Number line(s)

benchmarks, 301–302

to compare decimals, 329

to compare fractions, 299–301

to convert units of measures, 214, 215–218, 223, 227, 228

fraction on, 299–301, 315

mixed numbers on, 300

represent data on, 220

Numbers

compare, 10, 13, 257, 258, 297–298, 336

composite, 192, 194

decimal, 325–327

decimals on a number line, 329

even, 58, 192

format

expanded form, 8, 14

standard form, 8

word form, 8

fractions on a number line, 299–301

grouping, 17, 19

identifying, 7, 11

odd, 195

ordering, 258

patterns, 7, 195

prime, 192

reading, 11–12

representing, 3–7, 220

rounding, 8, 14, 21, 99, 141

Secret Code Cards, 7, 11, 329–334, 334

writing, 8, 12

Numerator, 251

O

Obtuse angle, 359–360, 367–368, 371, 382, 387–388, 395

Obtuse triangle, 363–364, 367–368, 387–388

Order of Operations, 161, 163, 183–188

Ounce, 225

P

Parallel lines, 379, 381–382

Parallelogram, 387–390

rectangle, 231–234, 236, 385–386

rhombus, 385–386

square, 233, 385–386, 401

Partial products, 69

Partitioning, 212

Patterns

extending, 195–196

in fraction bars, 252

in multiplication, 57, 193–194

growing, 196

numerical patterns, 195

Perimeter
    of a rectangle, 231–234, 236
    same area, different perimeter, 233
    same perimeter, different area, 233
    of a square, 233

Perpendicular lines, 380–382, 396

Pictograph, 177

Pint, 227–228, 235

Place value
    chart, 7, 333
    comparing, 10, 13
    dot array, 3, 85
        hundreds and thousands, 3
    drawings, 4–6
        hundreds, 3–6, 56
        ones, 3–6
        tens, 3–6
    grouping and ungrouping, 4
    groups, 55–56
    identify, 7, 11
    to millions, 11–12
    model hundreds and thousands, 3–8,
        11–12, 75–78, 95–97
    money, 325
    name, 7, 11
    patterns, 7, 11, 57
    read, 11–12
    rounding, 9, 14
    Secret Code Cards
        decimal number, 333, 334A–334B
        whole number, 6A–6D, 7
    tenths and hundredths, 330–336
    to thousands, 3–8
    ungrouping with zeros, 27
    write, 8, 11–12
    zeros in, 27

Place Value Drawings
    models, 3, 4, 6, 56, 67–68

Polygon Cards, 396A

Polygons. *See also* Geometry.
    classify, 395–396
    compose, 387–392
    decompose, 387–392

Polygon Cards, 396A
quadrilaterals, 383–386, 387–390,
    395–396
triangles, 364–368, 387–392

Prime number, 192

Problem Solving
    addition and subtraction, 36–37, 165,
        165–166
    comparison, 172, 173–176, 183, 277
    decimals, 332
    fractions, 269–271, 277–282, 304, 319
    hidden information, 38, 81
    measurement
        intervals of time, 220–222
        liquid volume, 218, 228
        mass, 218
        money, 37–38, 77–78
        perimeter, 231
    multiplication and division, 92, 100–101,
        275–282
    multistep, 40, 79–82, 146, 183–188
    Situation and Solution, 145, 165–166
    too little information, 80
    too much information, 79
    two-step, 181–182
    whole numbers, 275–282, 282
    word problems, 36–37, 82, 102, 165,
        235–236, 271, 282, 304
    write problems, 70, 128, 132, 145–146,
        173, 177, 183, 262, 265, 271

Problem Types, S8–S12

Product. *See also* Multiplication.
    estimate, 89

Product Cards, 46A–46J

Properties
    Associative Property
        of Addition, 22
        of Multiplication, 54
    Commutative Property
        of Addition, 22
        of Multiplication, 54
    Distributive, 69

© Houghton Mifflin Harcourt Publishing Company

Index

Properties of Operations, S7

Puzzled Penguin, 38, 82, 90, 100, 130, 134, 139, 166, 176, 186, 216, 258, 261, 268, 270, 278, 297, 301, 310, 317, 372, 392, 399

Q

Quadrilateral, 383–386, 387–390, 395–396
  parallelogram, 385–386, 387–390
  rectangle, 231–234, 236, 385–386
  rhombus, 385–386
  square, 233, 385–386, 401
  trapezoid, 385–386, 387–388

Quadrilateral Cut-Outs, 386A

Quick Quiz. See Assessment.

Quotient, 117. _See also_ Division.
  estimate to check, 141
  three-digit, 121
  two-digit and four-digit, 125

R

Ray, 352

Remainders, 117–120, 143–144. _See also_ Division.

Right angle, 354, 355–360, 368–372, 380, 387–388, 391–393, 395

Right triangle, 363–364, 367–368, 387–388, 391–392

Rounding
  to any place, 14
  to check quotients, 141
  multiplication, 65, 99
  to the nearest hundred, 9, 99
  to the nearest million, 13–14
  to the nearest ten, 9
  to the nearest thousand, 9, 99

Rounding rules, 9

S

Scalene triangle, 365

Simplify
  expressions or equations, 161
  fractions, 311–314

Square, 233, 385–386, 401

Square centimeter, 232

Square inch, 231

Square meter, 238

Square unit, 232–233

Square units, 54

Standard form, 8

Strategy Check, 16

Subtotal Method for Addition, 17

Subtraction
  angle measures, 371
  checking, 30–31
    by estimation, 32
  comparisons, 173–176
  difference, 32, 173
  estimate differences, 32
  estimate to check, 32
  find mistakes, 31, 32
  fractions, 259–262, 281–284
  money, 37
  real world problems, 30, 32–33, 34, 36–37, 40, 165–166, 173, 174, 175, 176, 182, 185
  related to addition, 29–30, 164
  from zeros, 27–28

Sum, 163

Symmetry, 397–400. **_See_ Geometry, symmetry.**

T

Tenth, 325, 329

Terms, 161

Time, 219–222
  add and subtract units, 221–222
  elapsed time, 221–222
  units of time, 219

© Houghton Mifflin Harcourt Publishing Company

Be an Illustrator

Illustrator: Josh Brill

Did you ever try to use shapes to draw animals like the lemur on the cover?

Over the last 10 years Josh has been using geometric shapes to design his a nimals. His aim is to keep the animal drawings simple and use color to make them appealing.

Add some color to the lemur Josh drew. Then try drawing a cat or dog or some other animal using the shapes below.

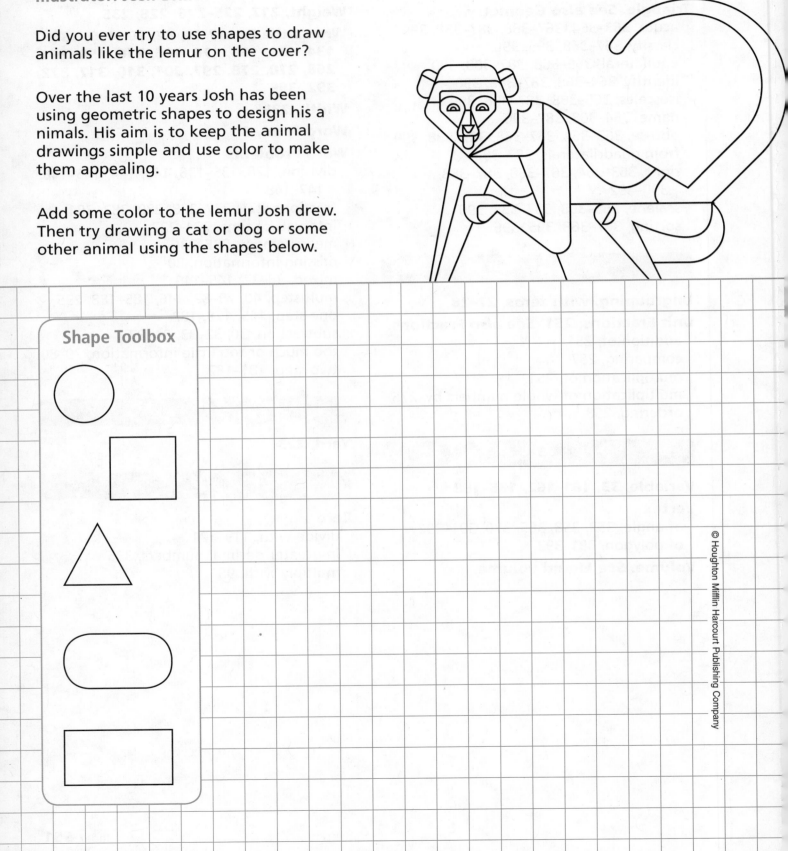

Shape Toolbox